PC Master Race

A beginner's guide to PC gaming.

TABLE OF CONTENTS

INTRODUCTION

If you're starting this book, you have to make a heartfelt pledge.

You pledge that from this point forward, you will put your loyalty behind the glorious world of PC Gaming. You will endeavor to explore its many secrets, and learn its many skills. You will accept it as part of your daily life, and you will rest easy in the blessed fact that you are now a part of the glorious PC Gaming Master Race.

As a part of this race, you have, at your fingertips, absolutely anything and everything that the gaming world has to offer. Unlike console gamers who have to jump across different hardware to get their gaming fix, all you have to do is boot up your trusty PC to get your dose of satisfaction. Unlike the others who have to contend with different platform-specific marketing gimmicks, your shining sword will cut through all unworthy expenses in such a grand manner that the broke onlookers could only ask how. Your citizenship in the PC Master Race frees you from corporate slavery, allowing you to pick and choose which rig and game you want to play, all according to your budget. No more forced upgrades or threats of total obsolescence. No more being left out. No more questioning whether the grass is greener on the other side.

I am Raul Jimenez, and I shall be your guide towards making the most of your alliance with the Master Race.

I am an avid gamer and a best-selling writer, from the Estados Unidos Mexicanos. I am the author of *Mexislang* and *The Gringo Guide to Moving to Mexico*, as well as the *Chicano*

Jrs. children's book series. This time around, I am turning my attention to that one thing I know and love — PC gaming, in all its finest.

Press Any Key To Start_

So what's up with PC gaming, anyway?

In order to really see its magic — to see how the PC Master Race dawned to rule over everything that is gaming — it's necessary to trace the history of personal computers as a whole. Here's a little stripped-down trip down memory lane — one that started with labcoat nerds fiddling with vacuum tubes, and ended with couch geeks tearing through more computing power than we used to get on the moon.

1822 - Charles Babbage was steampunk before it was cool. All the creative steampunk art you know will pale in comparison with what this granddaddy from England tried to do with steam. With the government's purse behind him, he tried designing a steam-driven computer that can calculate number tables — the conceptual forerunner of today's tech marvels. The device itself failed, but Babbage's ideas made their way into the structure of the first working computer built around a century later.

His idea of a steam-powered calculator was improved upon by Alan Turing, who in 1936 envisioned a device that is capable of computing *anything* that can be computed. The notion of the modern computer was born.

1937 - Things start solidifying. The idea of the "solid state" computer was born this year. Up to date, all attempts at making computers used moving parts such as shafts, belts, gears, and the like. An Iowa State University Professor named J.V. Atanasoff attempted to make a machine that does not use any of these, thereby chancing upon the next great technological innovation: vacuum tubes, which act like switches that signal the 1s and 0s.

This development saw its climax with the ENIAC — the Electronic Numerical Integrator and Calculator. Created from 1943 to 1944, this was the first-ever digital computer and is powered by a whopping 18,000 vacuum tubes. That's 800 square feet of primitive machine. In comparison, the UNIVAC (Universal Automatic Computer) which came a couple of years later occupied only a little under half that space and used only 5,000 vacuum tubes. All considering, it's a pretty big technological leap, but we're still a moonshot away from profitability.

During this time, the computer was pretty much nothing but a government tool — used for 1 part scientific investigations and 99 parts warfare. Computers like the ENIAC had been instrumental in bringing the Allies victory during World War II, by allowing them to break German and Japanese coded messages. These folks were playing one massive game with these computers, only they cost real lives and there's no respawn.

1952 - The first PC game starts ticking. Fancy a game of Tic-Tac-Toe? The first-ever computer game called *OXO* was created by Alexander Douglas. This is remarkable not only because of its implementation but also because its host machine, the EDSAC (Electronic Delay Storage Automatic Calculator) was among the first computers to be able to store information in its memory. Before then, computers can only compute. Now, they can remember where the players planted their Xs and Os.

1958 - The computer chip was born. Back in 1947, Bell Laboratories invented the transistor, which replaced the fragile bulk of vacuum tubes. This became the stepping stone for the next greatest thing in the digital revolution — the integrated circuit, which paved the way for the modern processor.

The boost in processing power provided by computer chips gave scientists a little leeway to give us some nice-to-haves — the mouse, the GUI, and one of the first operating systems (UNIX) to name a few. Introduced in 1969, UNIX was to be the base of many future operating systems. Home PC users weren't loving its slow and unfriendly interface, though.

1962 - Gaming went to Space. Before the OS wars, the browser wars, the console wars, and all the other wars... there was *Spacewar*, the first-ever video game to be featured in a tournament (to be held in 1972). This was the template upon which many later favorites, such as *Asteroids* were based on.

1973 - No more walls. The Ethernet is created by Robert Metcalfe, paving the way for networking. It was also during this decade that the computer started inching away from its government and business nature, on its arduous way to becoming truly "personal". Two models were of great note — the Apple II, released in 1976, and the Altair 8080 released two years earlier. The Altair was the testing ground of a certain operating system written by two nerds named Paul Allen and Bill Gates. The glorious PC Master Race has seen its dawn.

And yet it was Apple II that has the distinction of hosting the first truly revolutionary computer game. *Ultima I* was released in 1981, making its mark as the first-ever role-playing game, and the first-ever open-world game. Here you play as "The Stranger" who seeks to destroy the "Gem of Immortality", in order to free the people of Sosaria.

Despite the possibility of the "Personal" Computer, most computers (due to cost and the technical experience required to operate them) were confined to office spaces where they were used for business-related processes. The introduction of *WordStar* in 1979 made word processing a breeze, while the advent of *VisiCalc* a year before it made computers indispensable for organization, accounting, and similar uses. Not many people needed to do that at home, though, so a PC in one's bedroom is still a very rare sight.

1981 - Windows begins its victory march. Windows as an OS got its first big debut when it was paired with the first-ever IBM personal computer. IBM's "Acorn" computer had a color monitor and a primitive Intel chip. It was influential in coining the term "PC".

This MS-DOS incarnation was still a few steps away from the interface we knew, and it was visually outdone by Apple's Lisa computer which had its own GUI. In response, Microsoft created its own GUI under the name that will strike awe in the hearts of everyone from that moment on — Windows. Thanks to its glorious interface, both geeks and non-geeks were able to unite under the banner of home computing. The computer became truly personal, at last.

Later that decade, the groundwork for the future of PC gaming was laid out. The first Enhanced Graphics Video Card was released in 1987. Just a year earlier, the 32-bit architecture was introduced, marking the time when PCs gained processing power similar to the mainframes of yore.

The 90s - No turning back. The 1990s was a daring, colorful, and sometimes dangerous barrage of technological developments. HTML and the Internet were both formally born then, with a massive surge in web-based companies (the DotCom bubble) and the proliferation of the first worms and viruses. The first Pentium microprocessor was also born, along with games that exploited its processing power — *Doom, Command & Conquer, Alone in the Dark 2,* and *Descent* were just some of the titles that heralded the age of computers as gaming machines.

Multiplayer also finally caught a break in this decade. Mplayer and GameSpy were among the first to offer an online multiplayer solution in 1996, followed by Heat.net in 1998. Heat.net garnered fame for hosting the Heat College Internet Game League, which pitted players from over 1,000 colleges against each other in an *Unreal Tournament* and *Quake II* showdown. The cash prize was $5,000 — the granddaddy of eSports was born. This was followed by the World Opponent Network in 1998, which made multiplayer painless for more games like *Half-Life, Counterstrike*, and many more. Valve would later acquire WON, which became a keystone in its development of Steam. The days when multiplayer involved knowing the other person's IP address and connecting to their computer directly over dial-up became just a distant and bitter memory.

Before the turn of the millennium, another massive development fast-tracked the future of PC gaming — the introduction of WiFi as a wireless Internet solution.

The 2000s - The Future has arrived. PC technology and gaming as we know it was shaped in this decade. Windows XP was introduced in 2001, the company's swift and deadly response to the Mac OS X. It was even improved with the release of Windows 7 in 2009.

6

The first modern online games came in the form of online poker, and just a few years later Valve brought us Steam as a one-stop-shop for all our gaming needs. That same year in 2003, AMD released the first 64-bit processor that allowed PC owners to tap into even more power (while also birthing the bloody Intel v AMD war). This allowed the release of even more landmark games, from the sandbox classic *Minecraft* to graphically-intensive RPGs and MMORPGs. It was also this decade that eSports fully established itself, and that virtual reality started becoming... well, a reality.

What's interesting is that, just as the computer evolved from being a room-sized contraption that can only play Spacewar to a baseball-sized mini PC that can play a stripped-down version of your favorite MMO, we may not yet be seeing the end of PC and gaming development. Back in 2016, scientists have successfully created a reprogrammable quantum computer, and in 2017 the mad scientist arm of the US government (the Defense Advanced Research Projects Agency or DARPA, whose predecessor birthed the Internet) started research into using *molecules* as computers. Pretty soon we'll be wirelessly interfacing with a PC smaller than the head of a pin, and still powerful enough to bring us into virtual realities. What a world it would be then! *Ready, Player One,* here we come!

The PC Versus the World

Now, let me address that question that's at the back of everyone's mind. The history we have traced has painted the PC as an all-around device, that can do pretty much anything you want it to. In contrast, we have consoles — specially made and finely-tuned devices that are made to excel in nothing else but gaming. How does the PC beat them all out? I will spend the rest of the book explaining the fine details of the whys and hows, but let me give you a quick lowdown of why being in the PC Master Race is the best decision of your gaming life.

Budget. Of course, it's all about the economy. *Everything* is about economy. Everyone wants to make the most of their hard-earned dollar, and it's the PC that's best positioned to do just that.

Let's start with the obvious — your machine itself. It's not worth it talking about games if you don't have anything to game with, so it's your rig that matters most. And of all the devices money can buy, the PC is the most budget-flexible of all. You can start with the most basic setup, just enough to get a decent framerate, and upgrade later to a lean and mean gaming machine. You don't even have to upgrade your device wholesale — with a little planning, you can go slow and steady until you build your dream machine. A new processor here, a little more RAM there, a new graphics card after a couple of years — that's much less painful on the wallet than having to keep up with the latest Xbox or PlayStation or whatever else have you. Additionally, you won't have to replace the whole device if something goes wrong. Anyone who has experienced the infamous Xbox Red Ring of Death outside the warranty will know what I mean. In comparison, the Windows Blue Screen of Death can be fixed with either a workaround or an inexpensive hard drive replacement.

And then there are the games themselves. The paywall on a PC is MUCH thinner than its console counterparts. Steam sales are just one (but admittedly big) part of the picture — generally, PC games are in for stiff competition, so market forces dictate lower prices. Heck, you could even get top-notch games for free or a steep discount without looking around too hard.

And because a computer is primarily a networking device, you can leverage the power of the Internet to hunt for amazing deals. Anywhere from third-party vouchers, to "flavor of the week" freebies, to bundled-software — seek and you shall find. Even the game devs themselves join in on the fun, giving away old classics as free downloads as a publicity stunt for sequels. The only free thing a console gamer gets is the monthly game that comes with his subscription, which isn't free at all.

Speaking of networking and expenses, have you ever thought of how dumb it is having to pay extra just for multiplayer? The age of dedicated and paid multiplayer networks has come and gone, as we have seen. Now, multiplayer just *is*. And yet console makers charge extra with their "Gold" and "Plus" subscriptions just so they can play with someone else! If that's not highway robbery, I don't know what is.

Variety. As you shall see later, being a PC gamer lets you play pretty much *anything*, regardless of the game's original platform! Thanks to the ubiquitousness of the PC, any self-respecting developer would release a native PC variant of its big games. And even if they don't, there are always emulators — software that lets you "house" a different console in your PC (more on this later). Thanks to emulators, you can play not only games from other consoles but also from other eras! Fancy a little *GoldenEye* from the bygone days of the Nintendo 64? Now you can! The versatility of a PC's input and output even allows you to use various controllers, to complete the experience.

And even if your PC does not have enough oomph for emulation, or you simply don't want to go through the trouble, PC gaming still wins hands down when it comes to the types of games offered. The open nature of the PC as a development environment allows those really creative indie developers to go gaga and bring us awesome titles. The input options also matter — while playing a first-person shooter feels second nature using a keyboard and mouse, it's just not the same with a controller. Heck, *anything* feels second nature at a PC, such is its familiarity (except maybe fighting games). This allows for the proliferation of game genres on PC that would feel really odd on a console.

Technical savvy. Console gamers love to tout the fact that consoles "just work". And to an extent it's true. It's hard to go wrong when all you have to do is plug in the device, load up the game, and work the gamepad (never mind the myriad of options in various nooks and crannies, for those who want them). Compare this to a PC, where you can do pretty much anything — and where pretty much anything can go wrong if you're unlucky.

But put another way, the PC is the home device for many, and anyone who has experienced how to install a program has all the requisite skills needed to game on a computer. On the other hand, each console has its own interface and its own way to do things — transferring your familiarity from one platform to another isn't that easy. Compare this to a PC, where how you use a computer in your daily life is all you need to game.

In a way, the technical skills needed to game on the PC are just as flexible as the gadget aspect. Anyone can just launch a program and play, no problemo. Those who like to dance on the bleeding edge can, however, fine-tune everything according to their preferences. This includes everything from the hardware to the software, from the control to the visuals. Like in building a rig, you can start off with just basic gaming and work your way up the learning curve to fine-tuning your graphics and connecting multiple monitors and peripherals to up your game. While consoles generally need less technical savviness, they are also *very* restrictive should you decide that basic gaming just isn't cutting it anymore (and, believe me, that time *will* come).

And that brings us to the next advantage that's PC-exclusive...

Mods! Gamers are a creative flock of nerds, and they're never just passive consumers — they churn out content that don't disappoint! You won't have more than a small slice of the fun if you're a console gamer, however. Only the PC Master Race will ever experience the full-blown of a modded game, whether it's something simple like a costume change or a surprise multiplayer experience, or something more intricate like whole new levels and sometimes even whole new stories! To be sure, many console games have mods. Game publisher Bethesda (of *Doom* and *Fallout* fame) is zealously pushing mods, with the Nintendo Switch mods of *Doom* offering some smooth gameplay. But there's just no competition in the number of mods between PCs and consoles. PC modders don't need the nod of publishers for their creations to be shared with other users, unlike the current situation with consoles. From simple interface changes to complete graphics overhauls and even gameplay-changing variants, PC modding has it all.

In the end, gaming is an expression of creativity. And what better way to do that than to take something good and make it better and your own... or just take it and take it apart! No gaming life is complete without the fun (and sometimes absolute bananas craziness) of mods, and that's something most console gamers will have difficulty understanding.

Throughout this book, we will be tackling each of these aspects in greater detail. By the end of this book, you would have gained a full understanding of the PC Master Race and you will also find your place in this glorious realm. Are you ready to take the first step? Let's go!

CHAPTER 1: The Cost of PC Gaming: Finding your Hardware

Towards the latter part of this book — when we're neck-deep in technical stuff and all related mumbo-jumbo — you will learn how to get your own gaming PC, either pre-built or DIY. But for this part, I'd like you to be able to set your expectations (and your budget) by giving you the payoff for joining the PC Master Race.

Most online reviews say that consoles are potentially much cheaper than PCs when it comes to gaming since you only have to buy the console and the controller, and precious little else. A PC, in contrast, has almost a dozen moving parts that can all be swapped.

Now, let's put a number to that, shall we?

These days, decent console gaming comes only through a PS4/Xbox One or later. A pre-owned PlayStation 4 comes at just under $200, while a brand new one still costs anywhere from $300 to $400 (sometimes higher) depending on the edition. An Xbox One costs around the same. These are old devices, mind you, and were originally launched in 2013. Should you grow tired of them or need something with a little more under the hood, you can't just upgrade them to get the latest features. You need to buy the next-gen consoles, which as of this writing can fetch a price as high as $500.

In contrast, a refurbished Dell PC with a quad-core processor, 8GB of RAM, and a 500GB hard drive cost only a little over $100. Okay, maybe this build is a little too stripped down (it can game, but not really well). Then how about a custom-built gaming PC with an Intel i5 processor, 16GB of RAM, a 1TB hard drive, and a 2GB nVidia Geforce GT 1030 graphics card? This budding beast is well-equipped to handle most of the modern games, and as long as you're not looking to make gaming your life it's good for a few hours of hard keyboard-and-mouse pounding every day. And its cost also hovers just around $500, like the consoles. What, outgrowing that too? Then take out the parts and swap them for something new, and you're back on the frontlines.

It's true that PCs have a lot of moving parts you need to take into account when gaming. It can be daunting and complicated, and when you don't know what you're doing (or where to find stuff) it can also be pricey. But this is a blessing and not a curse of the PC world. We are at that age when technology evolves at such a fast pace that it's really hard to keep up. Consoles offer a turnkey, cut-and-dried solution for a gaming fix, but they don't really age well. Heck, I can remember the time when you were the cool guy if you've already upgraded your PlayStation to the PS2. That was until the Xbox arrived a year later, then the Xbox 360, Wii, PS3... you get it. PC gamers don't have that problem — if their current build can't support the latest release, they can just pick and choose which parts to upgrade. And while some of them can get notoriously expensive, replacing the processor, RAM, or graphics card is typically less expensive than buying a new console. All you need to know is how.

Simply put, on a PC it's all about choice. When you're buying a console, you're biting gaming company products hook, line, and sinker. These products don't even give you much by way of customization, except maybe hard drive size and a couple of fringe features that don't really improve the core mechanics of gaming. In a PC, everything can be fine-tuned.

Your kind of game may not even require those high-end components, and you can make do with just a basic build — i.e. the one you probably have today.

The Wide Spectrum of PC Gaming

Since PCs — in any form — are a necessity for daily life, I'd wager you already have one at home. Maybe it's a laptop you use for some light browsing and other tasks, or maybe it's a beefier build that you use for work or business. All these can be used to game!

Let me clarify one thing though. When I say "PC", I mean it in the historical sense of the word. That is a personal device that runs on Microsoft Windows. "PC" is to Windows as "Mac" is to Apple (Linux is just Linux). So any personal device you have that runs Windows is a PC, and you can use it as your springboard into the world of PC gaming. Whether you're just testing out the waters or starting a commitment, you already have basically all you need to experience the magic.

But in the off-chance that you don't have your own device yet, or you want to get another one for any reason, what are your options? The possibilities are endless — here's the spectrum of devices you can start with.

Netbooks. If you had your computer first as a student, chances are you have a netbook. Maybe it's the classic laptop-like netbook or one of those 2-in-1 touchscreen devices. By nature, a netbook is a small, lightweight laptop that is still bigger than a phone or tablet. It doesn't have much power and is built only to handle lightweight tasks and Internet-based processes.

Because it's lightweight in every way, netbooks can only handle the most basic of games. You're not limited to boring rounds of Bejeweled, though. Some classic games, from arcade ones to older MMORPGs can still run in netbooks. Browser-based games should work okay (though more graphics-intensive ones may occasionally lag). Basically, so long as you're not loading huge open worlds or anything with lots of things going on at once in the graphics and action department, you should be good. Depending on its specs, your netbook may even be able to handle emulating a different console. We'll get into that in the latter part of this book.

PC-on-A-Stick. These ultra-portable devices are built for one thing only — to serve as multimedia centers that can be plugged into the HDMI ports of your TVs, turning them into smart devices. They are built with traditionally low-end hardware, but they still have just enough juice to game at the same pace as netbooks. Not recommended for anything other than a casual jaunt through games, but if this is all you have you can still squeeze in a little bit of fun!

PCs-on-a-stick and netbooks may shudder and quake when faced with any modern game, but they shine when it comes to loading emulators (so long as you don't load anything beyond PS1). They can also load older games such as *DoTA*. There are lots of fun and resource-friendly games out there that can run on hardware slightly more high-tech than a potato, and we'll be exploring some of those later.

Later on, we will also talk about how to optimize the Windows OS for gaming, so you can use even low-end netbooks and PCs-on-a-stick for basic gaming. The PC Master Race, after all, does not discriminate among its citizens.

Laptops. By far the most common form of the PC, offering the best mix of power and portability. And I'm not taking "power" lightly — there are many laptops that have enough power to run even the most graphics-intensive games.

That said, the average Joe's laptop is often powerful enough to run both basic games and even some mid-range games at scaled-down settings. What's cool is that almost all PC games have graphics settings and other options that can be tweaked to make it friendlier to low- to mid-end devices. I once played CS: GO (minimum settings) on a laptop with a decidedly low-end Intel N3450 processor and no graphics card. It lagged in many instances, but it worked smoothly enough for me to bag my fair share of kills.

That said, not all laptops are ideal gaming machines since not all offer the primary advantage of PC hardware — upgradability. While netbooks are mostly transient devices that were meant to be replaced with a laptop or desktop down the road anyway, laptops can stick around for a long time depending on your lifestyle. And many laptop manufacturers nowadays offer devices with internals soldered together, so you can't replace them unless you know some electronics yourself. Even laptops with upgradable RAM may leave you stuck with the same processor. If you're thinking of settling with a laptop as your go-to gaming rig, try to find a model that allows you to upgrade it.

Micro PC. This is a new thing that's yet to become a trend, but if things go smoothly for the few dedicated manufacturers who produce them, Micro PCs might just work.

A Micro PC is essentially a laptop that can fit into your purse. It has a full keyboard operated mostly by your thumbs, and a trackpad or tracking dot (think the Lenovo/IBM ThinkPads). They also have a screen that is the size of a large phone, and either folds into or slides out from the keyboard.

What's amazing with these Micro PCs is that they pack around the same firepower as a low- to mid-range laptop. That means you can load your favorite (casual) game here and take it with you anywhere without lugging around a laptop. While it's impractical to actually play with the awkwardly small keyboard and screen, these PCs can be connected to an external monitor and peripherals, which gives you a full-sized experience — something that tablets and smartphones can't boast of.

Another reason I'm including Micro PCs in this list is because of the trajectory its latest development is taking. As of the time of this writing, GPD (one of the leading makers of Micro PCs) has recently launched a crowdfunding campaign for a gaming-oriented Micro PC powered by an Intel Tiger Lake processor. While this isn't top-tier hardware, the desired product (called the Win 3) boasts enough hardware for some serious gaming. Additionally, this Micro PC offers console-like controls — it's like the bastard child of a PC and a console, which is in a category of its own! Keep an eye on these prototypes as you make your journey through PC gaming.

Desktops. And finally, the overlord of all PC gaming — the trusty old desktop. It may not be as portable as laptops (even though some processing units are now so small they're practically pocket-sized) but they offer the ultimate PC advantage: near-infinite customizability.

This is where the money really is in PC gaming (pun intended). You can spend as much (or as little) as you want with your gaming rig, and if you want you can also make money out of it (streaming, esports, or any other creative way you can think of). PC has the biggest selection of games, and the biggest level of support thanks to the ever-increasing ranks of the PC Master Race. The amount of customization you can do is also mind-blowing, with builds that have price tags on par with a car. No kidding — the 8Pack Orion X2 (among the most expensive gaming PCs today) costs upwards of $40,000. On the other end of the spectrum, you can get a working refurbished unit for just around $50, and build from there.

PC gaming pretty much started in the US, where most of the biggest computing developments happened. Back then, stateside games were either digital translations of real-life games (such as Pong, or the aforementioned Tic-Tac-Toe). Electronics and programming geeks sat in their workstations, making creative use of the languages and processing power of the time, slowly turning the PC into an entertainment system.

And then, the Japanese game developers — the undisputed gods of viral titles during this time — turned their attention to the PC. At first, there were only PC ports of console games, but soon enough PC-only games were released. Then the gaming environment as we know it today was birthed, and we started getting parity in the release of titles.

Whatever desktop you have now should be capable of some measure of gaming. Even really old systems that came from 15 years ago would be able to run some old and fun games or some games that don't really require full-blown setups.

Think smaller titles like *Undertale*, basic platformers, or even visual novels.

If you don't have a PC but you're planning to buy one mainly for gaming, you would have to plan around the recommended system requirements of the game you want to play (or at least the minimum system requirements if you're good with reduced performance). Stick around for step-by-step instructions on how to do this, just a little later on.

Optimizing Windows: One Size Fits (Almost) All

The thing that ties this massive array of devices we have covered is that they all run Windows. That means outside of hardware limitations, they all should have pretty much the same behavior when it comes to games. And Windows is a great host OS for gaming because it offers a lot of opportunities for tweaking, so you can get the most performance out of any hardware you have.

Plus, Windows is the golden standard for software development nowadays. Here are just some of the few advantages Windows (especially Windows 10) has over any other software:

The Latest DirectX. You should have heard about DirectX — either through a random search or an even more random error message when you tried to install something on your PC. DirectX is a set of instructions that allows games to interface with your computer. Among the many things it does is to let the graphics card access your CPU, therefore availing of its processing power and allowing the game to run more smoothly.

Up until Windows 7, DirectX11 is the name of the game. This DirectX version (and all those below it) allows your PC to link up the graphics card and one core of the CPU at a time. This is frankly useless now that we have multi-core CPUs. Windows 10 arrived with DirectX12, however, and blew that out of the water — now the graphics card can talk to more CPU cores, greatly improving your gaming performance. Additionally, those with discrete graphics cards can now tap into the latent extra power that lies sleeping in their integrated graphics card built into the motherboard.

If you think that an additional core doesn't make a difference, think of it this way — DirectX12 games have a performance increase of up to 300% over DirectX11 ones. Plus, DirectX12 games also consume less power, which is great for those who game on the go.

Windows has always been on the cutting edge of DirectX development, so you can rest assured you'll get the latest version for your gaming satisfaction.

The Best Computer Graphics. Windows is the yardstick for all types of applications, and it's the same for the gaming world. Not surprisingly, it's also the same for hardware developers.

One of the main problems other OSes encounter is hardware compatibility. Simply put, all types of hardware are primarily made to work with Windows, and other OSes are just an afterthought. This is very true for graphics cards, which test primarily on Windows 10. Win10 is also the way to go for those who want the latest graphics drivers and other graphics-related optimization — which is pretty much every gamer out there. Better graphics cards and drivers translate to better framerates and overall performance, as Windows

10 is built in order to better be able to handle related processes.

The Speed of the Latest and Greatest OS. Even if you install Windows 10 on an old machine, you'll experience the difference in speed. It's like breathing new life in sluggish hardware. Install it on a machine with up-to-date specs, and you'll experience a different level of convenience compared to other operating systems.

Windows 10 is built to be fast. Boot-up times are drastically reduced, and multitasking is greatly improved. Thanks to this, windowed gaming is faster and snappier, which means you can Alt+Tab your way into and out of your game and not get caught up in lag. This is what multitasking means!

Finally, if you still insist on being a dual citizen and juggle being among the PC Master Race and the console plebeians, Windows 10 also allows you to access your Xbox Live content on your PC, as well as stream your Xbox activity thanks to the integrated Xbox App. A more relevant nice-to-have is the Game Bar feature, which allows you to record video and take screenshots, control your audio source and settings, and monitor your performance specs (RAM and CPU) while gaming. There's also a feature that lets you chat with other gamers.

Now, despite its friendly familiarity, Windows is still a very complicated OS — the product of thousands of corporate hours of development. If you've ever tried fiddling with Windows' settings, you would have known it's a fairly daunting task with its myriad of options, if you don't exactly know what you're looking for. At the very worst you would mess up your registry or some other essential part of your

OS while blindly following an online tutorial, and you'd end up with the Blue Screen of Death the next time you boot up.

In this section, I'll give you the lowdown on what settings to change on Windows, and why. This way you'll get a feel of how Windows gaming works on the OS side, also giving you an introduction into the tech stuff we'll be diving into later on.

First things first - Not All Windows Are Created Equal

For all our love for Windows as a gaming platform, it's still far from perfect. For one, there's a whole host of Windows Editions (12 of them for Win10) that have different specs. If you bought your PC with Windows preinstalled, you most likely have either the *Home* or *Pro* edition. The Home Edition has the least bulk since it is mainly targeted at consumers who don't need advanced encryption and all the extras that the Pro Edition offers. Performance-wise, the Pro Edition allows your device to handle as much as 2TB of RAM while the Home Edition only lets you go up to 128GB. On paper that's a world of difference — but let's face it, who really has more than 128GB of RAM? Unless you have a job at NASA or CERN or any bigwig companies, there's absolutely no reason to rack up that much RAM!

If you bought your device second-hand from an office garage sale, you might have one that has the Enterprise edition installed — a more powerful, but still heavier Windows version. If you're unlucky, you might have bought a device that has the extremely restrictive Windows S Edition, which was already phased out but still lingers in pre-owned machines. This edition does not allow the installation of third-party software (like your games), and you would have to buy your own copy of Windows that you will then have to manually install.

The point is, some Windows versions will have additional features that might hamper your gaming experience. The steps in this chapter will cover features and options that are available or applicable to all Windows devices. Your specific device may have other settings up for tweaking, but you will have to do a little extra digging.

That said, here's how you can tune up your Windows OS to prep your machine for gaming.

Stop runaway background processes. As mentioned, Windows is not perfect. One of the things it does poorly on is handling background processes, even if this aspect has improved drastically over the years. This is the one aspect that other operating systems can claim to beat Windows over, especially the ultra-lean Linux distros.

Still, Windows is very customizable. This means despite all the auto-pilot that goes on under the hood, you can still make your device run faster by manually limiting background processes.

Background processes refer to programs that take up RAM and CPU in the background even if you are not using them. Antivirus programs, for example, can run scans in the background and take up precious processing power even without visible windows. Chat apps and various clients may do the same, as can some browsers. PCs with robust specs can take the strain pretty well, but those with lower-end devices will greatly benefit from clearing these background processes.

The easiest way to see all running processes will be to run your b (simply search for it from the search bar beside Start). Pay attention to the programs that take up a lot of CPU and RAM, which are listed in the first and second columns of the interface. Make sure you're not using the app in question — if that is so, right-click the app name and close/terminate/kill it.

Remember that these background processes are here for a reason (most often for background syncs). Closing them will cause your app to shut down completely. Doing this on chat apps, for example, means you won't be able to receive incoming messages. This is why you should kill apps sparingly. Windows has its own way of app management, and manual intervention is only necessary if you're trying to squeeze the most out of your machine when gaming. Also, a word of caution — if you don't recognize the process name, don't kill the app! You don't want to accidentally close a vital part of the OS. If things go haywire, hit that restart button and make sure not to touch that app again.

Even then, this is not a cure-all for a sluggish PC. You'll find that some apps will restart even after being terminated. To put even more of the PC's processing power into your game, you can pair this technique with Win10's Game Mode. This will dedicate more of the system resources to the game so that it runs more smoothly. At the same time, it takes care of Windows' own background processes such as restart notifications and driver updates. To start Game Mode, simply search "**Game Mode**" under Start and click the "**Turn on Game Mode**" search result. Alternatively, you can go to **Settings > Gaming > Game Mode**.

Note that in some weird instances, Gaming Mode may interfere with the normal function of your game (ironically).

If you're experiencing issues, flip that switch back to Off and make do with the Task Manager method.

Disable Animations. Windows is not just meant to be user-friendly, it's also made to be pretty. That means there's a lot of animation effects going on, from the quick fade-in when you hit Start to the transparencies when you work with windows.

These animations are nifty eye candy, but on lower-end systems, they can take up a significant slice of the pie that is your system resources. At full blast, they can noticeably affect loading times. Disabling them is the way to go if you want to slim down your system as much as possible.

To do so, follow these steps:

> **STEP 1.** Hit Start and go to **Advanced Settings**, under the Control Panel.
> **STEP 2.** Under the **Advanced** tab, click on **Settings** and head over to the **Visual Effects** tab.
> **STEP 3.** Here you will see a list of all animations under **Custom**. You may pick and choose here depending on your preference, but if you really want the most performance you can untick everything except these two:
>
> - Show thumbnails instead of icons
> - Smooth edges of screen fonts
>
> **STEP 4.** Once done, hit **Apply**, then **OK**.

After this, it's time to dive deeper into your Virtual Memory settings:

> **STEP 1.** Again in the Performance Options dialog box, click the **Advanced** tab right beside Visual Effects.
> **STEP 2.** Go to Virtual memory, and hit **Change**.
> **STEP 3.** Do the following in order:

- Find **Automatically manage paging file size for all drives**, and untick the option.
- Click your hard drive from the drive selection window right below it (mostly the C: drive).
- Click the **System managed size** radio button, then click **Set**.

> **STEP 4.** Click **OK** at the bottom of the dialog box. Also, hit **OK** at the bottom of the Performance Options dialog box.

This should prompt you to restart your PC, and it should reawaken snappier than before!

Unlock the Ultimate Performance setting. As mentioned, Windows 10 was made to be both user-friendly and pretty, not to be a lean, mean performance machine. It's the difference between a pimped up ride and a barebones race car. Still, that does not mean you can't tap its full potential — if you're willing to dirty your hands a little bit in the command line.

Accessing the Windows **Command Prompt** is as simple as a search from the Start bar. Mouse over the result, and on the right-click **Run as Administrator**. This will open the familiar (and oft-dreaded) Command Prompt window with all its white text on black background splendor.

Type (or copy-paste) the following code into the blinking cursor:

powercfg -duplicatescheme e9a42b02-d5df-448d-aa00-03f14749eb61

This is a code that allows your PC to "unlock" the Ultimate Performance setting, which will tip your computer's settings to full-on beast mode. Once you hit enter, a Power Scheme message announcing the advent of Ultimate Performance will grace your Command Prompt.

To access this Ultimate Performance setting:

> **STEP 1.** Click Start and search **Power Plan**.
> **STEP 2.** Click on **Choose a power plan** in the resulting settings, and switch to **Ultimate Performance**. This last option may be hidden under the downward pointing arrow to the right.
> **STEP 3.** Afterward, click **Change plan settings** beside Ultimate performance, and switch all four dropdowns to **Never**.
> **STEP 4.** Head to **Change advanced power settings**. Go to **Wireless Adapter Settings > Power Saving Mode >** and change **On battery** and **Plugged in** to **Maximum Performance**
> **STEP 5.** Under **Processor power management**, make sure all entries under the **Minimum processor state** and **Maximum processor state** are 100%.

Once done, click **Apply** and **OK**. Under your Power Plan settings window, click **Save Changes**.

And voila! You have just uncaged the latent beast that lies in your PC! Do **NOTE** however that if you are doing this on a laptop or a similar device, it will significantly increase your PC's power requirement. Either remember how you're doing these steps so you can reverse them when needed, or refrain from doing these changes at all if power is an important concern. Or just make sure you know where all the power plugs are, and bring an extra-long charging cable.

Setting games to run on Ultimate Performance. The Ultimate Performance setting can also be applied to Graphics Performance, which is another important factor in making sure you get the optimal gaming experience. Windows 10 has a built-in Graphics Performance preference that allows you to choose what power options will be applied when you run a certain game. As a plus, this can also be used for non-game programs, so if you need to squeeze more power for any function then this is an option. Here are the steps you should follow to do this:

> **STEP 1.** Click Start and search for **Graphics Settings**. Click the relevant result.
> **STEP 2.** Under the app preference dropdown, choose **Classic App**.
> **STEP 3.** Click on **Browse** and choose the game that you want to add to the list.
> **STEP 4.** Once you add the app, it will be loaded into the setting and options will appear on the lower-right side of your screen. Choose **High performance** and save the preferences.

After this, the settings of your game will be enhanced to make the most of what your hardware has to offer.

Note that this isn't something that you should be doing for every game and program that you have. If your game runs fine on regular settings, adding them to this setting will just overburden your computer unnecessarily. If everything is on high priority, just imagine the wear and tear you're submitting your PC too!

Upgrading your Graphics Drivers. Speaking of graphics... For the most part, drivers get updated automatically and in the background — unless you manually disabled this, or unless Windows is encountering an error. However, if you have a discrete (i.e., separate, not built-in) graphics card, you may need to do manual updates. Graphics card manufacturers often release updates that make their products perform better when handling specific games or applications. This comes in really handy if you're playing the latest titles since most updates tend to boost their performance.

The steps needed to update your graphics card drivers will depend on your manufacturer. Often, these cards will install an icon on your taskbar that you can launch to see update options. If that doesn't work (or if you don't have such an icon) simply head over to the website of your graphics card manufacturer and download the latest package available based on your graphics card model. If you're not sure what model you have, simply click Start and search for **Device Manager**. Click the first result and you will see a list of PC components. Click the dropdown button next to **Display Adapters** and you will see your model listed.

Disable autostart for High Priority Applications. For gamers, boot-up time is very important. No one wants to wait several minutes before the PC is primed and ready to launch your game! But that's exactly how long it takes for PCs with lower-end hardware when autostart is enabled for high-priority applications.

High Priority Applications are resource-consuming programs that run in the background, even when their interface isn't active. You have already encountered these in our little trip to the Task Manager earlier, but this time we're going to try and nip them in the bud. Aside from improving overall PC performance, it will also help improve your boot-up speeds noticeably.

Here are the steps needed to disable High Priority Applications upon boot.

> **STEP 1.** Launch the Task Manager by right-clicking the taskbar and clicking **Task Manager**.
> **STEP 2.** Click the **Startup** tab, and look at the last column that says **Startup Impact**. Right-click all those programs that say **High**, and choose **Disable**. Their status should change in the appropriate column.

You may ignore all those applications marked as Low and Medium, though you can also disable them if you need to free up more resources from your PC. Just remember, don't disable any program if you're not familiar with it! You may end up disabling something important.

Once the changes have been completed, you may safely exit the window.

Turn off other eye-candy. Earlier we turned off animations and other visual effects, which tend to steal a lot of resources. If you want to pare down your PC even further, it's possible to turn off some nice-to-have features that are more eye-candy and minor conveniences than deal-breakers. These include Notifications, Multi-Tasking, and Focus.

You might be surprised at the inclusion of Notifications here, especially since it's that bit in your taskbar that tells you when something of note is happening in your PC. However, Notifications can also instantly call on the app that prompts it, leaving that app running in the background and hogging your resources. If you have other ways of checking your notifs anyway, you can just kill this wayward feature instead.

As for Focus and Mult-Tasking, these are just fancy names that allow Windows to automatically manage your on-screen windows so that they snap to edges, smartly, change focus, and all that. Unless you're a real fan of Windows' automatic window management — something that can be effortlessly done manually as well — then these features consume more resources than they are worth and can be disabled.

To disable these extra features, follow these instructions:

> **STEP 1.** Click start and search for **Notification & Action Settings**.
> **STEP 2.** To the left, you will see the **Notifications And Actions** tab. Click on it, and uncheck/disable everything under **Notifications**. This should gray out everything else on the screen, disabling them.

STEP 3. Proceed to the **Focus Assist Tab**, and disable all options here as well.

STEP 4. Head over to the **Multitasking Tab**, and disable everything there.

You may also go through all the other tabs and disable other features that you feel you won't be using. Be swift, be ruthless in culling all those unneeded features. Remember, your gaming convenience is at stake!

Finally, click Start once more and key in **Privacy Settings** in the Search Bar. Slide into the **App Permissions** section, and flip off the switch in **camera**, **microphone**, **location**, **email**, **contacts**, **phone calls**, and **voice activation** tabs. Aside from being constantly in the background, these settings can also compromise your privacy, so it's best to remove them while you're at it.

There is another set of notifications you might also want to turn off — in-game notifications, which can also open dozens of pop-ups that interfere with your resource utilization. At the same time, these notifications are tied to the recording feature of Game Mode, which is why you might *not* want to turn this off if you are into streaming or just recording your games. If you're not, then fire up Game Mode and head over to the **Captures** tab to disable all features there. While you're at it, you can also set the **Video frame rate** to just 30 fps where it won't burden your PC so much.

And there you are, you've taken your PC one step further towards being the lean, mean, gaming machine it was meant to be! Now just a little more tweaking and you're ready to go.

Make your mouse snappier. The mouse? Really Raul? But it's true — all gamers know that no matter how fast the mind, eye, and hand can respond, all would be useless if the cursor won't go where you need it to.

Since Windows is a multi-purpose OS, many of the settings built for the mouse are best suited for work other than games. Here are some options you might want to play around with, so you can make your mouse snappier and more responsive, based on your gaming needs.

The mouse settings can be found under **Settings** > **Devices** > **Mouse** > **Additional Mouse Options**. These contain settings such as pointer speed, precision, and more.

You can experiment on how fast or slow you want the pointer speed to be, with the default setting being the sixth setting from the left. For gamers, the Enhanced Pointer Precision tickbox will be of more note. When turned on, this setting will cause your cursor to move farther the faster you move the mouse. This is especially useful for those who have limited space in which to work the mouse, and it might also be useful to reach the various buttons you need to access when using most desktop applications.

But for gamers, muscle memory is a very important thing, and this form of mouse acceleration mucks around with that. It will be harder to predict where the cursor will be after any movement, and it can spoil your game. It's recommended that Enhance Pointer Precision be disabled, but it's still a matter of preference.

Note that different playstyles can mean different mouse settings. If you want to really zoom in on the performance, you can also tweak mouse settings in the game itself, as most titles offer low-level customizations of controls.

Adjust graphics in-game (and in your graphics card app). Aside from the support built into Windows to improve the performance of graphics cards, games also provide their own host of knobs and switches you can play around with to get the most performance out of your system.

Most games have various graphics settings available, with a general Low, Med, and High setting coupled with various particles, effects, shaders, and the like that can be turned on or off. For the best performance on lower-end hardware, you would want to turn most of these off, though that might just take out some of the fun from your game. Experiment, and you will find your sweet spot.

Graphics cards like Nvidia also provide their own settings optimizer (case in point the Nvidia GeForce Experience). These provide a few more settings that will allow you to tilt the balance towards better performance instead of better graphics. Choosing either will automatically set the game to run on optimized hardware settings.

Do regular maintenance. As the cherry on top of the icing, there are routine maintenance checks you need to do to ensure smooth performance.

Among the most important is making sure your hard drive isn't choked full by useless files — very important if you're on a traditional hard disk and not an SSD. Check and empty your Temp folder regularly (**Run** > **%appdata%** > **AppData** folder > **Local** > **Temp** > delete everything), since this is where most of the useless files pile up in.

Also, make sure your Windows 10 is always updated! It's a pain, I know, and Windows has a pesky way of initiating updates (or asking for a restart) at the worst possible time. But every Windows update is made to fix bugs and improve performance and security. An update is especially important if you have just installed your Windows, or if you have a new device.

While updates are mostly done automatically, you can check for one manually by heading to Start and typing **Check for Updates**. Click the relevant result, and you will see if you are up to date or not.

Finally, don't forget one of the most important factors that will make or break your gaming experience especially if you're on multiplayer — your network! You don't always have to update your plan to get better Internet, as a little rearrangement may be all it takes to strengthen your connection. If you're on WiFi, make sure you're getting a strong signal by being as close as possible to your router. If possible, go wired — Ethernet cables are cheap and easy to set up, so long as you don't have to cross long distances. Sometimes this little change can be all it takes to let your Internet speed catch up with your newly-pared down PC.

To wrap up this chapter, let me reiterate an earlier warning — don't fiddle with settings that you do not understand! There's a reason Apple decided to hide all the knobs and switches away from their users in their OSX releases — it's *so* easy to click the wrong option and break your system. If you're supplementing these tips with some stuff you saw online, be especially careful about tips that ask you to access various registry items and/or type in arcane codes into Command Prompt. Most such tips are obsolete and apply only to old Windows versions, or they do not have enough impact to really affect your PC's performance.

In short, not everything out there is a useful tip. If you don't understand exactly what you're doing, it's better to leave those settings be. After all, if you need those tips and you have a lower-end device, that means you're just starting your Windows gaming journey, and your PC is not yet even in its final form!

CHAPTER 2: Getting Into the Game: Games, Launchers, and the Kitchen Sink

Now that we've introduced you to how you can run a game on whatever Windows device you have right now, let's get to the real deal and answer the most important question: how do you actually get a game?

Physical or Digital?

The advent of PC gaming has pretty much changed the landscape of the game industry. Time was you needed to go to the store and buy a disc, whose content is then installed in your device. This went both for the PC and the console. But as PCs became increasingly connected, to each other and to the Internet, the idea of the digital game was born.

Digital games are different in that you don't actually own a physical copy of the game. Instead, you own the game's license, which means you have the right to download, install, and play it on your PC. This makes digital games so convenient — you can be the farthest away from any game store as possible and you can still get your hands on the latest titles. There's also the advantage of "pre-loading", meaning you can pre-order a game and it downloads the very moment it hits the market (provided you are connected to the Internet at this time). This puts you in the frontlines of gaming, eliminating the long line that used to form outside game stores in anticipation of big titles. And if you're looking for the indie variety too, digital is the way to go — small-time game companies don't always have the resources to go physical, so they depend on the Internet to show off their awesome work.

Time was (and you don't have to be old to remember this) that physical game copies stood on their own tier, with their own advantages. They can be cheaper, and the physical medium allowed you to store and lend games as you would any other item you own (i.e., without relying on the cloud). But today we live in a convergent world, and those advantages have been melded into digital copies as well. That is, when you buy a physical game copy nowadays, the box typically comes with a code that allows you to download the game's digital version. Yep, it's safe to say that technically, games are all digital nowadays.

There is one advantage, however, that pure digital games have — game streaming. Newer platforms like Google's Stadia and competing services allow games to be streamed to your PC without having to download anything. This instantaneous game experience comes in a subscription-based format and allows for a new way to game on your PC and all supported screens. No physical game copy can boast of being installable on multiple devices, so it's a win for the digital world.

For this chapter, we will be talking completely about digital games and digital stores. Despite some advantages that physical copies have, everyone, will admit that digital games offer unparalleled convenience and availability. Since we're talking to the whole PC Master Race spread out across all corners of the globe, we're going to depend on the sole resource that we know everyone has access to — the Internet.

Game Launchers: What they are, and which is the best

In the world of digital gaming, the game launcher is an absolute must-have. Game launchers act as the library which stores all your games, where you can choose what to launch and play. Think of game launchers as the app launchers in smartphones. Launch them, browse your games, and launch one. It's that simple.

Or, not really. Game launchers also double as game stores, where you can buy games. Think of them as your phone's App Store and launcher rolled into one. In reality, the game store aspect eclipses the launcher part since what would really matter is the selection of games you can get from a launcher.

There are several game launchers, most of them created by game development companies themselves. Of course, these types of launchers feature mostly games from the developer — Origin, for example, was created by EA Games and contains some of the company's best releases. There are others that are more neutral, such as Valve's Steam.

It's possible to have more than one game launcher on your PC. It's even possible to have them all, though it's not really advisable if your PC has limited resources. Each launcher takes up its own slice of RAM and CPU, so it would be nice to trim down your launcher selection to just the ones you really need. This next section will help you decide which is which for your PC gaming setup.

The Best Standard Game Launchers

Steam. Ahh, Steam. The undisputed god of all game launchers and game stores. Most casual gamers can't name any other game launcher, but they know Steam and its massive Steam Sale discounts by heart.

It's no exaggeration to call Steam the grand-daddy of all game launchers. First released in 2004, it was created by Valve Software, of *Half-Life* and *Counterstrike* fame. Old-timers will remember having to download that annoying Steam client just to launch *Half-Life 2* Today, all annoyance is gone as it has gained a massive array of games for all types of operating systems, from indie to AAA, from free to paid.

Steam also has a lot of other knobs to fiddle with. One of the standout features is the social media element, which allows Steam users to share their comments about the games they play. You can add other users as "Friends", and chat with them. You can even broadcast messages to a wider audience.

Steam is also the leader in terms of its game support. Aside from supporting otherwise gaming-incompatible OSes like Linux, Steam also supports mods and selling in-game items. You can gift games, and show off your game achievements directly in the program. Everything (games, reviews, *everything*) is also sorted neatly into a variety of categories, allowing you to find what you want or need fast.

And while Steam is a very capable and reasonably nimble store and launcher, "fast" isn't the best word to describe it. All its features tend to weigh it down. Yes, you can run it decently on a mid-range machine and even pull through on a low-end one, but it's not the best experience.

Still, I'd go out on a limb and say that Steam is the one game launcher that should always be in your bag. Even game devs recognize the massive footprint Steam has on the PC gaming industry, and most games are released here first. Its massive library (more than 30,000 games and counting) will be the perfect tool to find new games that suit your fancy. Don't rely on its recommendations system though — that feature is questionable at best. Also, it's the perfect tool to get discounts if you're cash-strapped — Steam Sales are to PC gaming what a pilgrimage is to the religious. Aside from periods when prices drop up to 90%, there are also periodic giveaways and contests.

Take note, though — Steam may be the king of the roost now, but it's gaining some serious competition. As mentioned earlier, various other gaming companies are venturing into the game launcher and game store business, and these big guns are slowly moving away from Steam in favor of their own platforms. Think of Netflix and all its clones cropping up. It's a shame that the villains of capitalism and consumerism have to tread on our sacred PC gaming grounds as well. They've already got us beat with DLCs...

Origin. This is one of those up-and-coming launchers backed by the corporate big guns. EA Games is one of the monolithic veterans of the gaming world, with a presence wherever you turn. They produced a few top-tier games, from *Mass Effect* to the *Battlefield* series.

Origin is a feature-filled client, and while it does not really compare to Steam it is a very good launcher. Its store has a lot of content as well, including non-EA games — though often these games only show up in the background, in the shadow of the promoted EA games. Still, among the game developer-backed game launchers, Origin is among the worthiest to merit an install on your PC.

Corporate backing is also the main force behind Origin's quality control. Its games are better curated, especially in comparison with Steam where a lot of questionable games have popped up. It is also among the most optimized game launchers on our list, with a fast interface and a really good background download speed. It also has basic cloud and social media functions, where you can Friend other players and display your achievements. The cloud-save feature is a must-have for many gamers, too.

Origin, much like Steam, also offers good discounts (though not quite as steep). One thing to look out for is EA Play, the platform's very own subscription service that offers a lot of good games for a monthly fee. Some of EA's best titles are locked behind this Origin Access paywall, but depending on how much you play you may find it's cheaper to just pay the monthly fees than to purchase the games. Subscribers also get early access to new premium game releases. There are two tiers to EA Play, the regular subscription, and a Pro tier. The regular subscription goes for $4.99 per month while EA Play Pro can be purchased at $14.99 a month for more game access.

Epic. Epic as a game launcher has a weird history. Much like Steam, it was initially developed for a single game (*Fortnite*) but it has since evolved into something bigger. Like the two previous launchers, Epic also has the standard bells and whistles such as cloud saves and achievements, but this is already its current form — those who tried it at launch will remember a buggy game launcher that sported exclusives even before it sported a search function.

The buggy software may have improved, but traces of its shaky beginnings are still there. Its review system isn't that good, even though its recommendations are pretty much on point. Compared to the heavyweights (like Steam, the gold standard) it comes out as minimalist. There are some issues with the way the store displays games as well, with pre-orders being put front and center instead of games you can actually download now.

Despite its quirks, Epic has a good selection of games and gives its users two free games every week (Thursdays) completely free. Top-tier titles are also given away in raffles. Epic also has exclusives that can make even non-believers want to give this launcher a chance.

GOG Galaxy. Let's move away from the modern stuff for a bit and take a side-trip down the retro lane (we're going on a deep-dive on this later, so watch out). For all those who started out looking for older games — like *SimCity 2000* perhaps — you might have heard of GOG or Good Old Games. Originally conceived as a hub for oldies-but-goodies, the retro collections have evolved into something better.

No longer just a place that lets you pick out games that can only run in an emulator, GOG Galaxy now offers a good lineup of games from indie publishers. Those looking for big-name publishers need not look here, but if you want a well-curated set of games from outside the beaten path then this may be your jam. GOG is pretty famous in its circles for running a tight curation ship, so could be sure you're getting the best of what this niche world has to offer.

Despite its old-school vibe, GOG Galaxy is not without its gimmicks. In an effort to convert gamers to its platform, GOG has launched the GOG Connect system that allows you to transfer your Steam games to the platform. This may be a good idea for those who have grown tired of Steam's features and interface, and want to try something more minimalist for a game launcher (which happens, trust me). The uncomplicated interface is good for those who just want to enjoy the pure joy of gaming without all its social trappings. But don't pass off GOG Galaxy as a mere dumbed-down game launcher and oldies game store. It has *The Witcher 3*! And let's not forget *Cyberpunk 2077* — GOG is backed by CD Projekt, the game's publisher, so it has their whole catalog there too.

By the way, if you visit GOG's site right now and look at the GOG Galaxy page, you will be shown something completely different — GOG Galaxy 2.0, the evolution of their client, and an aspiring all-in-one game launcher. The information above applies to their classic client, GOG Galaxy 1.2. As of the time of this writing, GOG Galaxy 2.0 is in open beta and offers a different set of features. We will be covering those features in the next section of this book!

Battle.net. Let's move to another launcher that first came to light because of a specific game. Battle.net was created by Blizzard of *World of Warcraft* fame and first started as a multiplayer option for those wanting to play the original *DOTA*. Over time, it too has evolved into a fully-functional game launcher with such heavyweight titles as *Call of Duty: Black Ops 4* and other games by Activision.

But being a Blizzard product, its finest points almost always relate to Blizzard Games. For that reason, there aren't many options in this launcher. That makes it pretty light if pretty boring feature-wise. Its strong suit is in its handling of esports-oriented games, such as *Overwatch* — there are pretty good in-client streaming features, and it's not the type to keep disturbing you with notifications time and time again.

Bethesda Launcher. While we're on the subject of niche game launchers... and as we've touched on how some companies have pulled their games out of Steam to give their launchers an air of exclusivity... let's also look at Bethesda which fits both descriptions.

Bethesda is little more than a client that launches and sells Bethesda games. You will be paying attention to it, however, since *Fallout 76* was only available here, as will be all future *Fallout* games (despite their predecessors being available in Steam). It's not all *Fallout* though, as it also carries *DOOM! Eternal* and *Wolfenstein: Youngblood* among other titles.

What's interesting is that the platform's development seems to be taking on not the heavyweight Steam but its partner in niche-ness, Battle.net. It has a streaming option to match, and the community option is also pretty much similar. It's not something many would recommend unless you're really low on resources or you really like Bethesda's games.

Bethesda has also taken on a new level of evolution lately — for more information, check out our entry on Xbox Game Pass below.

Ubisoft Connect. This is an evolution of Ubisoft's ill-fated and much-maligned UPlay game launcher. Not too long ago, UPlay was the laughingstock of the launcher community — most people who had it actually didn't download it, but it installed itself as a consequence of a Ubisoft game that was launched from Steam.

Not anymore. Ubisoft Connect has evolved into a decent launcher that, while still featuring mainly Ubisoft titles, is at least more serviceable. Downloading the client lets you access its "Free Weekend" feature where access to top-tier games is given for free for a limited time period. And because Ubisoft games span all gaming platforms, Ubisoft Connect also provides you with a one-size-fits-all digital games ecosystem for all your devices.

As part of their gimmick, completing challenges in Ubisoft Connect allows you to earn points that can be exchanged for in-game perks. There's also a subscription service called Ubisoft Plus, which allows you faster access to game releases as well as closed beta access. Basic social features are also available.

While Ubisoft has some nice features, being the top dog still remains far out of reach for one simple reason — the best Ubisoft titles are available elsewhere anyway. There's no real impetus for a person to install Ubisoft Connect... but if you're playing the publisher's games chances are this auto-installed anyway as the DRM management tool of their games. Old habits die hard, even for the gaming world.

Xbox Game Pass for PC. What's a console name doing in this list, you wonder? Well, this refers not to the console, but to the companion Windows app that Microsoft releases along with it. The Xbox Launcher is the second on this list that has a tie-in subscription tier the Xbox Game Pass for PC. Launching the app shows all your Game Pass games, and it's worth noting that the subscription's library is a pretty good one for the price.

Game Pass for PC sets you back $9.99 every month, but that scores you a lot of good titles and some additional discounts. Or, if you want, you can just leave the subscription alone and buy games for their regular price. Aside from being a launcher and a store, the Xbox app also has social (text and voice chat) capabilities that tie into your Microsoft account.

It's not the first choice for communication, but at least it's there.

Compared to many other launchers in this list, it's pretty above average. It's also getting better, since Microsoft has recently bought Bethesda, so the latter's games will now be available in Xbox Game Pass from the first day of their releases. There's still no word as to whether or not the launchers will merge, but that may be something to look out for in the future.

Performance-wise, it's also good — being a product of Microsoft, it integrates well into Windows 10. The interface feels like home, too, so you might want to check this out as your daily driver.

Itch.io. This may be a familiar name even to casual gamers. Itch.io has made a name for itself as the go-to for indie games, which can be downloaded directly from the web. In fact, the main idea of downloading the Itch.io client is as a way to rein in the whirlwind of disparate Itch-downloaded zip folders and .exe files that litter your Downloads folder.

The game launcher itself is slim and fast, thanks largely to the games it runs — they are almost always low-resource games, developed as they are by indie devs. This might be the lightest client on this list, and despite that, it offers a decent search and categorization feature that lets you find new and interesting titles.

Overall, it's still a pretty niche launcher — *the* launcher for those with few system resources and even less time and money to try out big games, mostly. But it's a good game store and launcher anyway, so give it a try and maybe you'll like what you see.

The Windows Store. Wait... what? That one place for downloads preinstalled in your PC that you don't actually download from is a game launcher?

Well, it is, if you want it to. Okay, it's got absolutely none of the trappings that the other entrants in this list have. No cloud saves, no social media, no streaming... nothing but the ability to download a game and launch it afterward (though really, you can just use Start for the latter).

The Windows Store is your go-to for all Microsoft games if you don't want to download any of the other launchers above. It's got decent titles, from *Halo* to *Minecraft*, from *Forza* to *Gears of War*. It even has *Ark: Survival Evolved* and a few more cool games. It also allows you to buy an Xbox Game Pass, so it can be a handy shortcut for when you want to dive into more Microsoft.

But don't expect much in terms of variety, as the Windows Store is chock full of smartphone clone games of dubious concepts and mechanics. It has no decent curation or recommendation system, so unless you know the game you want is in there, there's no use launching it. Except maybe for some really unique instances, such as if — for some nefarious reasons — none of the other launchers in this list would work for you.

So what's the best? Ask most PC gamers and they would say that Steam is the absolute best game store and launcher. But as always, it's a matter of opinion. I would say try them out and see which suits you best.

Of course, I'm not saying you should waste your time and try them *all* (though you could do that). Steam is always a go-to, but I recommend also trying Epic and GOG Galaxy.

Epic is great for those who want a sleek and fast launcher, with good content, giveaways, and great discounts. It's not Steam, but it's not far behind. GOG Galaxy, on the other hand, is a great launcher for those who want to explore the finer points of PC gaming. Think of it as your guide to expanding your gaming horizons, with its curation and its unique content. It's also a portal to the past, with its original collection of classics — anyone who has played *Neverwinter Nights* and its contemporaries could attest to the glory of this bygone era.

As mentioned, it's okay to have multiple launchers especially if your games are all on separate stores, or if you're just testing them out. However, there is an up-and-coming class of launchers with a different kind of aim. While they also act as storefronts for game exploration and purchase, their primary mission is to serve as an all-in-one launcher for all your games, no matter the platform. These launchers are heavier on the game organization front than in the rest of the traditional game launcher features, so they occupy a completely different class. For convenience, I am calling this class the "universal game launchers" because they place a premium on finding your other games and organizing them for a hassle-free launch experience. Meet more of them below!

The Best Universal Game Launchers

Now, don't get me wrong — the big guns like Steam support adding third-party games or those not downloaded from its platform. However, it's not the launchers' strongest suit, with quite a bit of manual labor needed. The "universal" launchers take the fuss out of the process by doing things automatically, so you just have to sit back and play.

GOG Galaxy 2.0. Some have called the second generation GOG Galaxy the potential "Steam Killer", and judging by how its development is going it's not too much of a hyperbole.

Of course, GOG Galaxy 2.0 is still a front for GOG's catalog of games. But it also supports scanning and organizing games from other launchers. It also supports crossplay with Steam, so you don't have to convince your friends to change launchers just so you can do multiplayer matchups.

GOG Galaxy 2.0 is also heavy on Internet-related features. When you're online, you can back up your game purchases DRM-free, so you can store them in a separate medium. The launcher does not need to be connected to the Internet to launch, and it also offers one-click rollbacks if you're not loving the latest game updates. Speaking of game updates, you can automatically update games (default) or go the manual route with a single preference change. An upcoming feature also allows you to stay in touch with your social stuff via in-game overlay, so you don't have to leave your game just to check notifs, messages, and requests.

Don't worry about bloat though — despite GOG Galaxy 2.0's many features, it still stays true to the optimization that characterized its predecessor. CPU and RAM optimizations are a part of each release, and it has the awesome feature of making every other feature optional. If you want just the launcher and nothing else, you can disable them — something other launchers should take note of!

GOG Galaxy 2.0 is still in the open beta phase, so there will be future rollouts to watch out for. But if the app continues its development the way it is doing right now, it should be on every PC gamer's radar!

LaunchBox. While we're on the subject of launchers that evolved from old-school roots, let's also take a look at LaunchBox. Originally a DOSBox emulator launcher for old games, this program has since evolved into a highly-configurable (read: tinkerer's dream) launcher. Settings can be changed at a whim, which means you can tune LaunchBox to be able to run on almost any hardware.

Automation, however, is not LaunchBox's strongest suite. It also scans games from other launchers, but there are a few issues when the game doesn't show up as intended. In this case, you can fall back to manually adding the game, and the process isn't much different from other launchers.

LaunchBox may not be the smoothest launcher in this list, but it's worth a try especially if you have some really old games that can't find a home in other launchers.

GameRoom. Once upon a time, Microsoft had its own project called Game Room that allowed users to collect copies of classic arcade games. The project had since died, but the name lives on in this (completely unrelated launcher).

GameRoom also supports emulators, so yes retro games still have their place. But even better, it supports games from all of the launchers we have discussed so far. There's also the option to automatically run custom arguments when launching a game, which is especially great for emulation so you don't have to manually set up flags.

While there aren't as many updates as there used to be, GameRoom remains a viable option for those looking for a good universal launcher.

Playnite. Playnite is among the youngsters of the game launcher industry, but it's no weakling. Its developers have polished the client to a level where its age doesn't show. The client also supports auto-scanning your device for all games installed from other launchers, and it also has a lot of standard features to sweeten the pot.

But one aspect of Playnite makes it very attractive to a group of people. It is open-source, which means it was built by a community of contributors who help make it an interesting rival for its corporate-backed competitors. This community ensures Playnite gets new updates and features.

The program has theme support as well as support for a variety of extensions. These extensions are fun since they allow the client to get new (albeit experimental) features on a pick-and-choose basis. The client also allows you to import your playtime from the Steam and GOG Galaxy clients.

Razer Cortex. So far we've encountered gaming launchers that are optimized to run smoothly on lower-end hardware... but what about one that can also optimize the games themselves?

Razer Cortex is one such game launcher. It does the job of finding and organizing games pretty well, and it has a host of other tools too. These include options to boost the game's performance and the system's performance overall. There's even a cleaner option that will help you get rid of all that junk on your device in just one click. After doing all the optimization in the first chapter, there's really not much need for these tools — but in case you ever need them, here they are.

Aside from all these, Razer Cortex brings a feature that once you get used to you'll wonder how you ever lived without. The launcher can automatically find deals on games, regardless of which launcher they use. You will be notified of these deals in time, so you can take advantage of them even if you're not using any other launcher. An app that scans both games and deals — I'll take it!

Photon. This is a weird game launcher for a specific reason — it's not free. It was, up to version 3, but since then its users would have to shell out extra if they want to load more than 5 games into it. Which is kinda scammy, given that there are free alternatives.

Is it worth the price, though? Photon has all the standard bells and whistles of any game launcher, but it also has a few unusual ones, too. One is being able to download patches even for older games and apply the patches automatically. This is done through Photon's own database, which makes it different from other launchers that can only patch the most recent games.

It's hard to recommend Photon for this alone, though, unless you really need that feature. Still, it's a good thing to keep in mind in case you have a few extra bucks and would like to try this launcher out.

Discord. Another "wait, what?" moment coming your way! Discord is popular even among non-gamers for being one of the best chat and voice chat services around, but since three years back it has decided to shoot for the stars and go against Steam in terms of services. Aside from opening up its own game store, Discord has also launched a "Universal Library" feature that scans your PC for games. These games are then automatically added to your game library, for a one-stop gaming solution.

And why not? Other game launchers are investing heavily in their social features, so it won't be weird for a primarily social app to take the opposite approach. So far Discord seems to be handling the transition right, despite a few flaws in the game search feature. Still, since most gamers already have the app installed, it won't hurt to try its game organization chops out as well.

Downloading Games Online... Sometimes for Free!

Of course, while game launchers-cum-stores are the go-to places for getting the latest and the greatest games, they aren't by far the only ways you can get your hands on a good title. In fact, there are even more titles floating out there in the vast cyber eddy we call the Internet than those lassoed together by game launchers. And even better? *Many* of these sites offer free or heavily discounted games all the time!

Still, it takes a bit of time and patience to find the best websites for downloading games, so I shortened the path for you with the following list!

IGN Beta Giveaway. Aside from hosting awesome gaming and pop-culture content, IGN is also one of the most popular sites where gamers download premium titles for free!

Members of IGN's Prime subscription get a host of content, from free indie games to beta keys that allow them access to content even before public release. Aside from beta keys (for the uninitiated, codes that allow you access to the beta tests of soon-to-be-released games), you can also get free in-game items. There are also sweepstakes and other promos.

If you're hunting around IGN Beta Giveaway, make sure to act fast — these promos close up as soon as the game hits the market, so there's always a time limit.

Ocean of Games. The title says it all! Ocean of Games is another gamer favorite, simply because it's so hassle-free. Simply search, download, and enjoy! The site compiles and releases all sorts of legally free games, from early access releases to older titles that have been given away for free by their devs.

The success of Ocean of Games has prompted half a dozen illegal (and dangerous!) clones of the site. To make sure you're on the right track, make sure you're on oceanofgames.com before downloading anything.

Humble Bundle. Ahh, one of the most well-loved game resources on the Internet. Why? Because you're doing good to the world every time you buy something from their service. The site hosts several giveaways and even has a forum (via a subreddit) for title requests. But it also offers discounted top-shelf games in a bundle (hence the name), and a portion of the proceeds goes to charity!

Humble Bundle hosts different games at different times, so you should make it a habit to check back to find the latest deals. It's also a plus if you're using Steam since there are Steam key giveaways every now and then. For those wondering, a Steam key is a verification code used to register a game you download for free on Steam — it's basically your license to the game, and getting a free Steam key means you get the right to play the game for free. The game download itself is done separately.

DLH.Net. Speaking of doing good to the world, we'd be remiss if we forget the longest-standing entry in this list: DLH.Net, where DLH stands for Dirty Little Helper. The name was a throwback to the time when the site posted tips on how to cheat your favorite games.

Today, however, the site has turned around to become a legit source of free games. Its large community welcomes new signups with free Steam keys, and they also give away keys from time to time.

My Abandonware. This site is dedicated to a special breed of games — those that have been abandoned by their developers, and can now be legally given away for free. And by Jove, there are *thousands* of them. This site does an awesome job of collecting and cataloging them for your gaming pleasure.

The site does not require any registration, so you can simply download and give the games a go. Some of the more iconic titles include the original versions of *Warcraft* and *Need For Speed*.

Steamgifts. Here's a site that is completely dedicated to Steam-related giveaways — from free games to in-game gifts! You need to sign up and link your Steam account for both your safety and that of the site's (substantial) community. This is so that scammers cannot game the site, and so that you can't win any games that you already own.

The site is run by its members, who sponsor the giveaways. Make sure to check the latest threads to see which games are being put up as freebies, as these can run out pretty fast.

r/freegames. Speaking of community, here is a subreddit that is dedicated to giving away free games and game content! There are several such subreddits, but this one has the most activity. Like the rest of the entries here, there are free keys being given out regularly, with random games in the bag. There are also in-game items, and the community also points to other legal free game resources every now and then.

While you're on Reddit, make sure to check out the official Steam subreddit since a lot of members of the community post there as well. You would get a few insider tips too, on where and when to scout for free or discounted games.

GOG. We've mentioned it earlier, and it's worth mentioning again — if you're not after the latest titles, you'd find some of the greatest classics and more here at Galaxy of Games. The site publishes the back catalog of various game developers, giving you an awesome and well-curated selection of freebies. Aside from CD Projekt which is the parent company of GOG, Ubisoft also has a long-standing agreement with the site to provide its older titles for free.

Giveaways from GOG typically last for around 48 hours, and a couple of times a year there are premium titles being given away for free. What's not to love?

Green Man Gaming. The great thing about online gaming is that country borders are virtually non-existent. Check out this multi-awarded UK-based game retailer that has thousands of games in its catalog, at great prices.

If you're not particularly looking to fork out a Benjamin for a few games, they also have monthly giveaways (again in the form of Steam keys). The caveat is that if you already own the game, you can't exchange it for a different title. You may still trade the Steam key for a different game from another fellow gamer.

Steam Communities. Finally, there's Steam itself. The platform hosts a thriving and supportive community, the likes of which include those who give away free games. You can simply do a search, but for starters, there's the Game GiveAway Group and the Free Games GiveAways. Both of these communities have more than a hundred *thousand* members, a shining testament to their contribution to the PC Master Race.

Cheaper by the Key: Online Resellers

We've already talked about gaming keys, and how you can get them for free online... but did you know you can also buy them?

Stay with me here because at this point there's a little (okay, *much*) more caveat than in the previous discussions. To help you understand the hows and whys of buying game keys, let's do an analogy. Let's say the game is not a game, but another commodity — like a car.

The car manufacturers like Ford, Toyota, and Honda are like game developers, who make the commodities to be sold. From the factory, the cars these manufacturers make will be shipped to their official storefronts, such as the nearest Ford dealership — these dealerships are like the game launchers we talked about earlier, which operate directly with the blessings of the manufacturers themselves (often branded after the developers, too). Because they are official extensions of the manufacturers, the brands have full control over pricing — the only reason why Steam has the capacity to drop its prices like hot potatoes during sales.

But you don't only buy a car from official dealerships. There are also private dealerships that score deals with car manufacturers, and they get products for sale as well. These are the retailers, which are likened to Green Man Gaming, Humble Bundle, and similar entities. Depending on the deals they get from the manufacturers, they can pass these onto the end-users.

And then there's that wild and shady car dealership two blocks down from your home, with its colorful trappings and loud music. Sometimes you can get a really nice purchase off this lot, but you also know that among the shiny displays are those of questionable origin. Was that car stolen or not? Maybe it was a giveaway that should not even be sold? Well, you can't really tell from here...

That last example is what we'll be talking about in this section — the resellers.

Replace cars with game keys and you pretty much have an accurate picture of how keys are bought and sold over the Internet. Resellers are like the Craigslist of game keys, where anyone who has a key can sell them. Like real-life resellers, prices here are very low, so if you can't find the title you are looking for in one of the resources we listed above then you can try here instead.

But again, you have to be careful who you buy from. A person can have any number of reasons why they want to part with a game key. Maybe they bought a Humble Bundle, but they don't feel like playing one or two of the games there. Maybe they just want to monetize the game key for a title they haven't played in a long time. Whatever the reason, once you buy the key, the rights to playing the game transfer to you and you can now register your own copy of it. Buy the key, download the game, register using the key, and you're off.

But because the key is a digital item, it is also possible to track its usage. Game companies are not supportive of the concept of key reselling, and while they don't really crack down on them, they are also ever-watchful of fraudulent buy-and-sell activities. Sometimes a person buys a key with a stolen payment method and sells it, only for the key to be deactivated when the payment method owner reports the matter. The poor buyer will then have bought a useless string of digits. This is just one of many examples of fraud that can happen in the conduct of buying and selling game keys, so you have to be careful.

To make sure this does not happen to you, make sure that if you dive into the world of resellers, you do your homework diligently. I won't be recommending any specific platforms as the "best" in this industry, for the sole reason that I don't want you to have the false idea that one platform beats out another in terms of the quality of its wares. Also, keep in mind that fraud does not really lie with the platform itself — it lies on the sellers. Just as Craigslist or eBay is not inherently fraudulent, you can still encounter fraudulent transactions there.

That said, here are two of the most famous resellers on the Internet. Note that I am not recommending these sites or vouching for them per se, just offering them up as a suggested starting point if ever you want to dive into reseller game keys. Evaluating the authenticity of the individual transactions will be your call.

G2A. Some time ago G2A became controversial when a publisher pointed to it as facilitating the sale of fraudulently-obtained game keys. For all that, though, G2A remains to be the most recognizable name in the field of game key reselling. Their site offers a wide array of keys across various genres, along with some "random" purchases that are like the gacha of the game key world. The price is in EUR, but they sell internationally so it's not difficult to make a purchase. You can even filter out the prices of their whole catalog depending on how much you're ready to spend.

G2A also has other goods aside from game keys, with everything from game peripherals to other sorts of household electronics. They even have toys and tabletop games, along with apparel. Whether or not you're going to buy, browsing their catalog is a satisfying experience.

CDKeys. Unlike G2A, CDKeys automatically localizes the site's prices so there's no conversion necessary. The site has lots of keys at bargain prices, across all consoles. They even have a cashback feature for frequent patrons.

The site features Daily Deals that cover various gaming platforms, offering many games at heavily discounted prices. If you're itching for the latest games, there's a New category that lists all their most recent offerings. There's even a section for upcoming games that are on a pre-order basis.

They don't nearly have the wide range of games that G2A has, but the game-concentrated content of the site may make it easier to browse for many. At the same time, the site offers ways to top-up for the most common online and gaming wallets, along with a wide variety of gaming options.

Because of the inherent risk in buying game keys from resellers, it is advisable to stick to the bigger names like the game launchers and the retailers. If you can't find your title for the price you want anywhere, though, then a trip to G2A or CDKeys may be warranted. It's debatable how these resellers impact the gaming ecosystem in the long run, but as long as you're on the legal side there's no problem.

Keep It Legal

Now that you have a hefty selection of sites from where to download games, here's something important you need to hear. There are a whole LOT more places to download almost all types of games you want. Yes, there are all sorts of torrent tracking websites that give you AAA titles for free, cracked, and modded even if you so wish. And given how prevalent they are and how easy it is to get them, it's very tempting.

But don't. For your love of the PC Master Race, don't! All those games we love so much take a lot of money and a lot of hard work. Millions of dollars get poured into those games, and hundreds of thousands of work hours are spent creating a work of art that you'd like to play. By pirating a game, you are not only doing something illegal — you're laying waste to all that effort and robbing the devs of any compensation for their hard work. It's a dishonor to the game when you know the person behind the game has been cut off from the fruits of their efforts.

So stick to legit, legal means, and play on with a clean conscience!

Other Legal-ish Matters: DRM and Denuvo

Now, I'm no lawyer. But aside from knowing that piracy is bad, I also know a couple of other things that all gamers need to know to stay on the legal side. If you've been around games for a time you might have learned of these terms as well — and you might even have learned to look at them with a smirk. But what are they, really?

DRM

DRM — short for Digital Rights Management — is not unique to the gaming world. In fact, it is a term that applies to all forms of digital media and is a means of restricting the access or use of copyrighted works. Pretty much all digital stuff that isn't free and/or open-source has some sort of DRM built-in.

The most common means of DRM is through the use of licensing agreements, a contract between the user and the content provider, where the user pledges not to do certain stuff (such as copy the game without permission). This is a binding contract, and to renege from it is punishable by law. So really, you might want to read that EULA the next time you install a game... but in reality ain't nobody got time for that!

Remember our talk earlier about how physical games can be lent and borrowed and digital games cannot? That's one of the biggest reasons why DRM has gotten such a bad rap in the gaming world. But it's a fact we have to live with — the convenience of digital gaming comes with such restrictions. And it's not specific to PC gaming either. Consoles have their own counterpart to Steam and its cohorts (PlayStation Store, Microsoft Store, etc.) and they all employ DRM.

If you're not wanting to lend or borrow games anyway, DRM shouldn't be a problem. No amount of DRM (or lack thereof) can affect gameplay. The system is merely there to deal with rampant problems of piracy, by checking if the player accessing the game is indeed the player who purchased and is licensed to use it. That's why a game downloaded through one Steam account can only be used for that account, and a game downloaded elsewhere cannot be used with Steam without a Steam key to verify such a license.

The other thing that marred the name of DRM forever was the overuse of some game publishers. The fiasco that was *Sim City* and *Diablo 3* readily comes to mind — these games required a constant Internet connection to play, even though you're not doing any networking or social stuff. This is because the game used the Internet to verify the player's license to own and play the game, which is too extreme and completely dumb. Thankfully publishers have long since learned, and these tactics are no longer used.

Of particular note, though, is the one true danger that DRM poses. Let's say that you are a loyal Steam fan, with a few hundred games legally bought and licensed from the platform. Thanks to DRM, these games can't be downloaded, clones, or backed up elsewhere — they are and forever will be connected to your Steam account. That's good, because should you ever switch machines or transfer to another place your Steam account is all you need.

But *what if*, through the sinister workings of fate, Steam poofs out of the gaming world? What if one day we just receive news that the platform shuts down? The DRM connected to your games is also connected to Steam, and you cannot use them without the platform. If Steam ever bows out, all your games will as well. While the situation is not likely, this type of DRM apocalypse has been weighing at the back of many gamers' minds.

That's why it's advisable to go DRM-free as much as you can. Sure, you can't help it if you want a game that isn't DRM-free, but it might be worthwhile to search for a DRM-free version of the game if it exists. That said, we have already introduced you to some of the best places to search for DRM-free games. GOG is the golden standard in this regard, with its GOG Galaxy offering the benefits of other bigshot launchers while promoting awesome DRM-free games. Itch.io is a great place for DRM-free goodies from indie publishers, while Humble Bundle should be your go-to if you want to look for DRM-free versions of your favorite titles.

For all the woes that DRM gives gamers, you'd be happy to know that it's only PC gamers that even have the option to go DRM-free. Console gamers have to be content with buying physical game copies if they want to escape DRM, but that has its own drawbacks. As you see, being a citizen of the PC Master Race has awesome perks!

Denuvo

As mentioned, the term "DRM" is an all-encompassing one used for all sorts of anti-piracy schemes. Some DRM methods are as simple as a quick license check upon game startup. Others, however, are much more sinister. Enter Denuvo, the most notorious DRM scheme to ever set foot into the gaming world.

Denuvo's full name is Denuvo Anti-Tamper, a technology developed by Austria's Denuvo Software Solutions GmbH. The technology has been around since 2014, and has been employed in several games. Basically, a game publisher can license Denuvo's technology and integrate it into its products, where it acts as the DRM to protect the game from piracy.

For publishers, Denuvo has some great advantages. First, it is (a little) harder to break than other DRM schemes, staving off at least some of the swarms of pirates trying to crack the games. In the industry, Denuvo is famous for promising the "longest crack-free release window" — which is just a fancy way of saying that they do the best job of preventing gaming piracy, at least until the hackers find a way around their system. Which they always do in under a month, anyway. And that means money for the publishers, as the longer the game goes on without being pirated, the more money they can make from people who buy the game.

Now, we already said that a legit gamer says no to piracy. So any technology that helps cut off pirates should be good, right? Well, not in this case. In fact, the advent of Denuvo has been met with an almost unanimous cry of pain from the whole gaming community — the legit ones even more than the pirates. You see, pirates can always wait for a game to be cracked and released. And while waiting sucks, at least it's free. For legit gamers who forked out money to buy and play, however, they would be demanding at the very least their money's worth of gaming experience. And that's where Denuvo falls short.

Officially, Denuvo claims that its Anti-Tamper software does not impact the game in any way. But real-world tests say otherwise. In several instances, gamers (and game journalists) have compared software running Denuvo and equivalent software without their proprietary DRM installed — and the difference is not just noticeable, but largely damning for Denuvo. In one famous incident, _Tekken 7_'s director Katsuhiro Harada directly blamed Denuvo for frame rate drops in the game's PC version. While this is not always apparent, the frame drops detract from the experience when performing various special moves. For those gaming on PCs with lower hardware capabilities, these drops can be the difference between winning and losing a match. Harada's comments have been verified by other players, with other AAA-titles running Denuvo such as *Final Fantasy XV* also receiving the same criticism.

Denuvo's ill effects often manifest as longer loading times, frame drops, and higher CPU and storage usage. The last part can be especially dangerous for those SSDs with limited lifespans, while the CPU issue can be detrimental to the battery life of laptops.

The public outcry that rolls in the wake of every Denuvo game have caused some publishers to update their titles, removing the meddling middleware and vastly improving game performance. Some anecdotal reports even stated that post-Denuvo games had their performance increased by around 50%!

Still, Denuvo is alive and kicking thanks to many game dev's belief that the longer it takes for a game to be pirated, the more money they can make. While this may be true, it is only a gamer's wish that such an anti-piracy software be made without as much impact on system resources.

By the way, Denuvo's Anti-Tamper software is entirely different from another of their products, the Denuvo Anti-Cheat. The latter is a different solution that allows devs to stop the use of cheat codes, drivers, and many other cheat methods gamers have come up with over the decades. The Anti-Cheat system does not impact games in the same way that Anti-Tamper does, and it is now available in Steamworks for devs to integrate in their games. The Anti-Cheat technology is arguably much younger than Anti-Tamper, though, and the company has promised that it will continue to evolve — hopefully, it does so in a different way from its bulky cousin!

All Those Extras

In the olden days, a game is just a game, and when you finish it, it's just a memory. That's why games with a great replay value are so highly-prized because each time you play it feels like the first time. Today, devs are doing that and something more. With a little bit of extra content, they can turn an old game into something completely new, potentially changing the way you play... for a price, of course.

Before we end this chapter, let's touch on two aspects of gaming that are simultaneously loved and hated by so many gamers.

The Slippery Slope of Microtransactions

So far we have discussed where to get games, both paid and free. Now let's head to a little corner of the gaming world to which many people don't even spare a second glance... and yet this corner has claimed countless hours of people's lives, together with their hard-earned savings accounts.

This is the little corner of microtransactions.

To say "little corner" wouldn't be demeaning it. By design, microtransactions are meant to pop up in the corners of your game, every now and then. Waiting too long? Here's a little purchase that could speed it up. Having difficulty in a level?

Have a pair of shoulder-mounted missile launchers — for a dollar. Looking too bland? There's a make-over waiting for your character... behind this paywall.

Game developers (mostly big-name ones, and sometimes even the indies) are inherently businessmen, and they're not really the type to release anything completely for free, solely out of the goodness of their hearts. Even if they don't cajole you every two frames to buy something, they will always leave that as an option. What's more, most of these purchases are fairly small scale so they're easy to get into. Surely you have a few cents up to a couple of dollars lying around, to exchange for a good sword? Good. Oh, just in case you're interested, there's a full suit of power-ups also available for about thrice the price that I'm offering you now.

The thing with microtransactions is that they're exceedingly attractive. Aside from the small price tags, the pitch is always made during a pivotal point in the game when you really could use an extra hand. Either that or at the point where you're starting to look more and more like a background character when sized up by your peers in multiplayer. With a few clicks, you can gain access to new weapons, a massive cut in the waiting time, or a new wardrobe.

And because it's so easy and attractive, it's been the go-to sideline of many game devs. No matter the game's genre, if there's any story or multiplayer involved at all, there's bound to be a microtransaction somewhere in the menu. In the various games I've played recently — *Rocket League, Fortnite, Paladins, Path of Exile, Warframe, Cave Story, Team Fortress 2, League of Legends, Dota 2* — the paid content feature just about as prominently as the free content. No one minds because a good free-to-play game

71

will always be free-to-play, and never pay-to-win. After all, as a player, it's nice to have the options to get stronger and better-looking in an instant even if you never use it.

Just make sure, though, that when you do use it, you use it responsibly. Because of the nature of these microtransactions, it's so easy to get enthralled in the experience of improving your character one purchase at a time that you forget *how much* you're already spending on it. If you have the dough and you won't need it elsewhere, then by all means splurge. But it's not uncommon for gamers to spend more than five times the price of the game just for microtransactions... and you can only imagine how many games they own.

Bottom line is, buy in-game purchases responsibly. Just to give you an illustration of just how much money gets spent on microtransactions, let's take a look at the late-2020 hit *Genshin Impact*. Now, you may love or hate gacha games, but it's undeniable that this game is pretty well-made what with a production budget of around $100 Million. Yet it was released by its dev for free... and it made the whole $100 Million back only *two weeks* after release. The culprit? In-game purchases for various upgrades and gacha pulls. While it's nice that devs can make so much money for their quality content, you don't really want to be that guy who spends thousands of dollars trying to get a character (true story). Or maybe you do... no judgment here!

DLC: Downloadable Content... or Dev Left out Content?

Speaking of money and quality content, let's talk about that other side of gaming that isn't quite as slippery as microtransactions, but just as rewarding/vexing depending on who you ask.

Let's take a short trip back to the older times again. Back then, games were just one big chunk of content, and unless you're a dev or modder you can't add more to them. The closest you'll come to having some new content will be in the form of sequels or expansions. But as the Internet became the norm for content delivery, publishers have started delivering game-related content even after the game has been purchased... sometimes for a price.

Curiously, the first documented instances of DLCs on PC gaming weren't for profit. Unlike microtransactions where a price tag is always involved, the modders of the late 90s used the Internet to distribute their own creations for free. Some devs eventually followed suit, and used the technique to keep their games updated and relevant (and their players hooked for a longer time).

But at one point down that road, someone realized that they could *sell* this content instead, and ride on the high that gamers experience upon playing. Of course, gamers would always want more of a good thing! So the concept took off, and today DLCs are often sold as "expansions" or "editions" that allow you to unlock something completely new. Unlike micro-transactions that don't really affect the fundamental flow of the game, DLCs do just that. Whether it's a new story, a new stage, or a new character, a DLC aims to give a fresh take on that game you just finished. Sometimes, DLCs contain purely cosmetic changes that players pine for anyway. This how some fighting games like the *Dead or Alive* series (and recently even *Tekken*) extended their play time considerably even after the final stage. Seeing those beauties duke it out in... uhh... "creative" new costumes is just a must-see! Of course some DLCs do provide for a different breed of curiosity, such as the additional trains you can buy for *Train Simulator 2000*. Onward, aspiring station master!

While this is great news for gamers, some game publishers have taken the idea to the extreme. Some DLC packs have been known to cost almost as much as the games themselves. And while they do provide extensive additions to the experience, many decry DLCs as an excuse for devs to leave out key portions of what should have been the whole game, remarketing them and making more money than is reasonable.

There's also the concept of "passes" or subscriptions that entitle gamers to regular releases of DLCs. What's controversial is that the content of these releases is not initially known to the public, so gamers essentially pay for something they can't see. This has caused many instances of discontent with subsequent releases, with subscribers accusing publishers of milking their games more than they're worth.

Still, DLCs are not all traps and treachery. Many devs provide free DLCs, with their only revenue coming from the ads attached to them, and the offer of micro-transactions that go along with them. This seems to be a much better way of handling things if only more devs adopt that line of thinking.

As gamers, we are not averse to paying for quality content. All we demand is that the experience be worth the price. Because of that, DLCs will always be a hot topic. When you're up and gaming you will encounter them, and you have to decide for yourself whether it's worth it.

Of Launchers and Mods

But don't turn away from extra content completely, as not all of them are made to divest you of your hard-earned savings. In fact, many of the best content out there are free and are made by none other than the zany minds of the gaming community. Sometimes these mods do something as small as correcting typos and fixing bugs (that for some reason the devs ignore), and sometimes they do something as big as transforming the whole game's looks and functions. Want to ride a giant chicken into battle on *Skyrim*? Check. Want to recreate Tolkien's Middle Earth war on *Total War Kingdoms*? Absolutely. Want to experience how *Half-Life 2* can deliver a compellingly rich and utterly suffocating horror environment? Oh yes. Want to mix *Doom 3's* engine with the *Thief* series' gameplay? There's a mod for that.

Earlier we talked about how mods have become some of the best features of PC gaming. I also mentioned how Steam has its own facility for managing mods, and this is through the excellent repository called Steam Workshop. Steam, and an app we'll be mentioning later called Vortex, have done the admirable job of organizing what were once disparate mods so you can find them all under one roof. Trust me, if you were modding in the early 2000s, your folders would be filled with lots of files you'll eventually be unable to make heads or tails of.

The Workshop is one of Steam's many community-driven corners, serving as its own mini version of Itch.io. Essentially, enterprising gamers and amateur content creators can upload, download, and vote for additional content for various Steam games. This content comes in the form of additional maps, skins, levels, and even artwork. Basically anything related to games can be seen here! The Steam Workshop is also available through your browser, so you can access it anywhere.

75

While some mods have the "free" price tag stamped all over the quality of the content, there are also premium mods for certain games. Payment goes to the mod's creator, so some have turned it into a sort of backyard industry, churning out the wildest mods for popular games. Make sure you read the text reviews to make sure you know what you're dealing with! Once you've chosen a mod in Workshop you can just hit the **Subscribe** button and the content will appear in your Downloads section. Once the download completes, the content will now appear in-game. You can delete mods (you'll want to delete some of the too-crazy ones, trust me) by going to **Your Workshop Files** in Steam and heading to **Subscribed Items**. Click on the **Subscribed** button again to unsubscribe.

Not Loving Steam? Mods Are Everywhere!

If you don't feel like trawling the Workshop for mods, you'll be glad to know that there are more (and arguably better) places for mods over the Internet! While none of them offer the one-click intuitiveness of Steam, they offer an amazing variety of gamer-made content to choose from.

Nexus Mods. Nexus holds some of the biggest and most complicated mods out there. And by complicated, I mean mods that change more than 10,000 elements of the original game in one go!

Nexus Mods are organized by the game, and the site currently has more than 1,000 games in its library. Big name RPGs like *Skyrim*, *Dark Souls*, *Mass Effect*, and more. There is also a dedicated mod manager (called Vortex) for download once you've created an account, which makes tracking and installing downloaded mods much easier. The manager also scours your drive for games already installed and tags those it supports so you can easily mod them.

The Nexus community is also bustling with activity, with over 15 million registered users and billions of files downloaded. If you're just casually browsing, there are recommendations in the form of spotlight features. The fact that the site also incentivizes great mods with cash prizes also draws out the best that the community has to offer.

Mod DB. While not as expansive as Nexus, this site is still worth checking out. Aside from thousands of available mods (most of them catered to older games such as *Command and Conquer* and *Doom*), the site also offers a place for mods to post blogs and updates about their works in progress.

The site also hosts one of the oldest Mod highlight campaigns anywhere, with the Mod of the Year awards running for the past 19 years!

Dedicated Sites. There are several sites out there that specialize in providing mods only for specific game types or titles. For example, there's **Minecraftforum.net** for everybody's favorite blocky open-world game, and **GTA5mods.com** and **GTAxScripting** for those who want to raise their respect levels in all-new ways. There's also **NoMansSkyMods.com** for those who want to explore the open universe with a twist. For MMO fans, **CurseForge** opens up a whole host of add-ons as well.

That said, sometimes it's just as well to browse Google results to find just the right mod you're looking for to add spice to your gaming. Make sure to visit the classics though, such as the original *Team Fortress* mod of *Quake* (yes, before TF became a game in itself) and the *DOTA* mod for *Warcraft 3*. Or simply go totally ape-nuts-bananas with *Garry's Mod* for *Half-Life 2*. Your game, your choice!

CHAPTER 3: Gaming Like it's 1999: The Rise of Emulators

Nowadays, most AAA titles are defined by groundbreaking graphics and jump-off-your-screen visuals. Sure there are still *lots* of games that focus on great stories, creative gameplay, and captivating characters, but for others, these factors play second fiddle in making the action on-screen as realistic as possible.

Back in the old games, though, it's all about mechanics. Sure that seems lame nowadays — almost every game genre has been explored and perfected — but there was a time when games stood out by doing what no other game does. This was the time of the classics, of the titles that created now-famous (and cliché) gaming tropes.

And because PCs were not yet gaming machines during this time, this was the time of consoles. Game publishers did not then have the concept of "cross-platform", and created titles exclusive to what was then the hottest consoles of the time... and we all know where that led. Nowadays these classic games — still worth playing, despite their age — have their creative souls trapped by hardware limitations. Ever come across a copy of the original *Ocarina of Time* or *Perfect Dark*, two of its generation's definitive games? That's great, but now you need a Nintendo 64 to plug the cartridge into. And if by chance you're hopping through classics (like in school, a gamer should be well-versed on the classics!) and are ready to dip into *Resident Evil: Code Veronica* for education on real-time 3D horror, you'd need either a Dreamcast or a PS2.

Except that you don't, thanks to PCs. Not PCs alone, mind you, but the *emulators* you install in them. An emulator is software that allows your PC to act as the device it is emulating. Installing a Game Boy Classic emulator, for example, allows your PC to imitate how a Game Boy Classic works, and also allows your device to read games meant for this handheld pioneer. Thanks to technology and the tireless work of several amazing people and communities, there is an emulator for almost all consoles of the past. The only exceptions are the more modern lineups, but there's always a project in the works for those.

The first game emulators appeared in the early 90s, with the release of the Family Computer Emulator in 1990 and the Pasofami in 1993. The NES console was a hot item during these days, and Pasofami was also released on Windows in 1993. These two represented the first trickles of the emulator floodgates that were soon to open.

Nowadays, emulators play a lot of roles in the gaming community. Of course, there's the basic role of acting as a time portal, allowing gamers to access games from long-dead consoles. They also serve as museums, allowing gamers to preserve old games whose publishers are not generous enough (or legally allowed — licensing issues abound in the gaming world) to work on a re-release. *007: GoldenEye*, anyone? It's a shame this revolutionary FPS never made it out of the N64. Emulators also act as new homes for the childhood games we used to play in the arcade, such as *Dungeons and Dragons: Tower of Doom* and *Alien vs Predator*.

What's more, though many emulators have advanced settings that allow for various customizations, most of them are simple and readily available enough that anyone can download them. This way, most of the games we love will forever be available, even if the consoles die out or even if the publisher goes belly up. While consoles have limited lifespans (we are in the 8th generation of consoles!), the PC Master Race is forever!

Emulators vs The Real Thing

Some console stalwarts would argue that emulating a game (and its console) is far from the real thing. To an extent, they're right. Not all emulation software is built to perfectly copy how the original consoles work. Also, there's the nostalgia factor of not just playing an old game but also playing it on an old console. You're only getting about half of that if you're sitting in front of a high-tech PC while playing an 8-bit game.

Still, emulators have a host of advantages that consoles can never have, such as the following:

Performance and Graphics upgrades. PCs, especially gaming PCs, have several times the processing capacity of consoles. Even a low-end PC has significantly higher processing capacity than most old consoles. This processing power can be leveraged to make old games run much more smoothly on PC than on their original homes.

Aside from faster load times and less sputtering in between scenes, PCs can also leverage the power of their graphics cards to give games a visual upgrade. While it's not really worth it to go 1080p on *Pokémon Red*, many a game experience can be greatly improved by utilizing the power of the modern PC. Try running something like *Xenoblade Chronicles* with an HD texture mod and anti-aliasing on, and you'll see the difference.

Patches and Features Galore. Patches and mods are a thing for emulators, and it's not hard to find homebrew versions of your favorite games with an extra feature or two. Maybe a completely new plot or stage even, if you're lucky! If the game's original language isn't to your liking, translation patches also abound to make sure you understand what's going in. This is heaven-sent for the game archeologists out there who want to try the older sim-like games (*Sakura Wars*, anyone?) originally published in Japanese, without having to guess what the cursor is pointing at.

And then the emulators themselves offer an amazing array of add-ons for your gaming convenience. There are means of debugging games and recording both audio and video. There are ways to speed past slower gameplay elements. There are settings for auto-save and auto-fire. There are even ways to go on online bouts when such technologies didn't exist at the time of the original! Online platforms (bundled in emulators) like Fightcade allow for multiplayer in such games as *Metal Slug* and *King of Fighters*. Other platforms like Slippi (for *Super Smash Bros. Melee*) allow for even more quality of life enhancements, such as replays and "rollback netcode" which allows latency-free multiplayer over long distances.

Cheaper overall cost. While buying or building a PC can be more expensive than buying *one* console, imagine having to buy various consoles to satisfy your gaming needs. While it's possible to buy some of these consoles from various places (online to garage sales) dirt-cheap, the fact that you're not getting a brand new unit means you won't know how long it takes before your console breaks down. Refurbished units are also available, but the price gets ratcheted up pretty steeply. Rarity can also increase the price — for example, a

TurboGrafx-16 can cost anywhere from under $200 to above $1,000 depending on whether it's over-used or never used. Tough luck if all you want to do is check out *Castlevania: Rondo of Blood* and you haven't heard of emulation.

It's also easy to forget that while consoles are not too technically complex (at least compared to a PC), maintaining them can entail significant costs. When one of them breaks down, you can't always just take them to the nearest electrician unless they know how to fix that specific console. If you need to replace parts, it's even harder. In contrast, since emulators are software, they're really hard to "break". Their host PCs are pretty easy to fix, and parts can be bought just about anywhere.

If you're all about retro and you're just starting out, it's also great to know that many emulators work excellently on low-spec hardware. You can literally buy a pre-owned sub-$100 PC right now and start playing on emulators without any significant performance issues. This makes entry into the world of emulation a breeze.

Overall Convenience. Let's face it, though... no gamer is really *all* about retro. From time to time you would want to sample the latest and greatest in gaming, while still taking an occasional dip into the classics. What is a gamer to do? PCs and emulators are the best solutions.

Console gamers argue that their way of gaming is much more convenient. Simply plug, load, and play — no configs, no setups, no fiddling. But then again, if you're on console, you get stuck with just one kind of convenience. It's the PC that really gives you *overall* convenience.

Sure, there are a few knobs and switches you need to play with to get some emulators running, but it's much easier to just launch various software on PC than change physical consoles. You can be getting hopelessly lost in Hyrule in *A Link To The Past* one moment, and getting purposefully lost in the same place in *Breath of the Wild* the next. It doesn't even matter if you're dipping your toes in games from different consoles of the past. There are multi-system emulators available that make switching emulated hardware a breeze.

Also, there's the problem with saving your progress. The original consoles weren't really good at handling saving (ancient memory cards, anyone?), and even then games can only be saved at specific points instead of on-demand. While that turns up the challenge, it can also be very frustrating — something that most emulations fix.

And finally, there's the matter of switching controllers. Consoles are never very flexible, and you'd have to adjust your fingers to whatever controller your controller comes with. On the PC, you can plug in literally any supported controller and get the same gaming experience all the time.

As always, however, it's not all sunshine and roses. There are a couple of drawbacks that emulators will have a hard time getting over:

Consoles offer perfect compatibility. Most emulators are homebrew stuff or the products of community-driven projects. As such, they are not officially supported and they contain compatibility issues every now and then. In contrast, a game built for a specific console will always run perfectly, so long as both the game and the console are working properly.

This is one of the few instances when the monolithic experience of console gaming has a real advantage. While emulators are always being improved, there are too many moving parts in both hardware and software to ensure perfect compatibility 100% of the time.

The nostalgia factor cannot be duplicated. When you play in an emulator, there's always the sharp pang of realization that you *are* playing in the emulator, instead of getting lost in the game as the developers had intended. There's just something different with experiencing the actual system by yourself — the experience of plugging in the wires, loading the game or cartridge, and watching everything come to life is just an irreplaceable experience. Retro consoles are a touchstone to the past, a more innocent time when it's okay to see pixelated graphics and non-AI movement. Definitely not something a casual (or even a pro) gamer would consider very important, but an experience worth having nevertheless. Massive plus if you have one of those old-school CRT TVs, too.

Of course, there's the unusual satisfaction that comes with collecting the actual games. It's one thing to have them stored in ROMs on your PC, robbed of their original bodies, and another to see them in all their old-school glory. The array of colorful cartridges and CD cases with their iconic game art is a thing to behold. It's a challenge as difficult as gaming too since there are lots of consoles and several games exclusive to each. That said, it will be a very expensive hobby — but if you have the resources, why not? At least physical copies have resale values.

Aside from these two factors, there's really no definitive reason to choose the real-deal retro console over the emulator.

How Emulators Work: The Soul of the Game

Earlier we've talked about how games are preserved by the advent of emulators. That's no exaggeration. Do you realize how many games had been completely lost due to various reasons until fans revived them by emulation? Several would-be franchise starters and genre-definers had disappeared inexplicably, only to resurface later on through emulation. One thing that comes to mind would be *Thrill Kill*, an unreleased EA game that would have been the first fighting game to be both ultra-violent and playable by more than 2 players. It took an incomplete leak and fan-made patches to recreate the game and give it new life.

In essence, preserving games through emulators is not that different from preserving ancient books and movies in digital format. All it takes is to extract the media from its physical shell and turn it into something accessible by a computer. For books, the text is extracted. For movies, the moving pictures and the sounds. For games, it's a little more complicated — the programming is pretty complex, and it's not always a straightforward affair.

There are two parts to transferring a game from a retro console to a PC. The first part is the emulator, and the second is the ROM. The ROM (Read-Only Memory, reminiscent of "CD-ROM" where most games used to be housed) is the soul of the game. It is a digital copy of all of the game's programming, packaged in such a way that it can be accessed outside of its physical medium. ROMs are also called ISOs, after the file format used to store data in optical disks. ISOs and ROMs are used by loading them onto the emulators — like virtual cartridges — which are in turn programmed to be able to read the bits and bytes contained therein.

Virtually any type of game can be contained in ROMs, making preserving a game easier than it was a couple of decades back. While it's true that not all ROMs are perfectly compatible with emulators, the ability to create them made it possible to save games from aging and dying along with their physical bodies. Come to think of it, it's really weird that it's possible to download digital copies of thousand-year-old books, while it's no longer possible to play DC's *Infinite Crisis* MOBA since its servers shut down in 2015. The latter's game code was not preserved and so it's forever dead unless a relaunch happens. The same thing happened (perhaps thankfully?) to the original 2010 release of *Final Fantasy XIV*. Compare that to *Club Penguin*, which was saved and rewritten by fans so it's still accessible after its servers shut down.

We won't be discussing how to create ROMs out of physical media (that's far too complicated) but suffice it to know that ROMs are easily available online. Fans have created dedicated websites where they "dump" ROMs of retro games, free for everyone to download. These dumps are accessible with a simple Google search — simply search for your game title and add "ROM" or "ISO" at the end, and you're good to go!

Wait... did you say free? As in *legally* free?

Well... it *is* free. Among the several conveniences offered by emulators is the fact that several hundreds of games are easily downloadable for free. Note that these ROMs and ISOs aren't as technically advanced as top-tier modern games, so downloading them is a very quick affair, allowing you to skim through many games in a short span of time.

But the fact that there are so many ROMs and ISOs floating around for free raises an important question — is their use in emulators even legal? Isn't this a form of piracy?

To clarify, the use of emulators themselves is not illegal. These pieces of software were not pirated off anything. Instead, they are the result of a long reverse-engineering process in order to understand the programming behind a specific console model. Once that's figured out, the people behind emulator projects code this process onto the program that you then download and install onto your PC.

Because they're legal, you can download and install any number or type of emulator on your PC without any fear that the FBI is onto you. It's also good to know that emulators are not only found in the gaming world but in various software development applications as well. There are even Android emulators that can be freely downloaded and installed. The fact that emulators being used for a wide range of applications speaks to their legal status. And it's not just conjecture as well — in the US no less than the Court has declared that reverse engineering a game console (and its titles) is encompassed by fair use laws (Sega v Accolade, 1992 — if you want to impress your friends). Of course, don't rely on this ruling for everything. In the 2000s the US has also passed various protection measures that cover the type of intellectual property used in game consoles, so rulings may change.

But we were just talking about the emulators themselves, i.e. the software you install to run ROMs. The game ROMs and ISOs themselves are a different story because technically, they were copied off the original game and thus are pirated. In a purely legal sense, downloading ROMs from the Internet means engaging in piracy!

"But wait..." I hear you saying. "Isn't this just normal right now? I mean, everybody does it, so isn't it legal?" Sadly, just because it's par for the gaming course, doesn't mean it's legal. Thankfully, just because you've done it, doesn't automatically mean you're in trouble. How does that work, you ask?

When a game is pirated into ROMs, the act infringes on the intellectual property of the gaming company. The said company then has the right to sue you, if they so wish. But how likely is it that a game publisher, says EA Games or Ubisoft, would come after you for downloading the ROM of a game they published years ago?

As it turns out, not very likely. It's always a matter of economy for these big brands. They are balancing two interests here... well, actually just one, and that's profit. But there are two sides to that profit — the profit they will gain if your piracy is stopped, and the profit they will lose due to the litigation.

Most pirates get away with their acts because they don't step on the profits of game publishers, so the latter feel no need to come after them. After all, most emulated games are really old ones that the companies no longer make money off. Pirate a newer game or cut into their profit, however, and you could be in for a rough time if they ever wake up one bad morning and decide to sue you. If they have the money to purchase Denuvo licenses and let their games take a performance hit just to stop piracy, you can be sure they have the money to file a lawsuit as well. The proof is a case won by Nintendo against a company (and its distributors) whose device allowed gamers to play their own pirated ROMs and homebrew creations through the DS. The cartridge-like device was able to bypass the console's security. Notably, the DS was still only 4 years old at this time and was still a hot item in the gaming world.

So how do you cut into their profit to get onto their bad side? Simple — sell an emulated game. When you do this, you are making money off another entity's intellectual property, which at any rate and for any reason is a really bad thing to do. This is why emulators and ROMs are offered for free online, in ROM dumps. Anyone charging for them would just be looking for trouble. There have, in fact, been those daring and foolish few who tried this and got hammered by the long arm of the law. That VPN and anonymous username didn't really do much to protect them.

So there you have it, the golden rule to not get in trouble when downloading and sharing ROMs — don't make money off them. Don't go waving your banner around either when you do it. Be discreet, keep your head down, and just be chill about the whole matter. So long as you respect these rules and stay away from the cash cows of gaming companies, you'd be safe.

An instructive anecdote on this matter is the case Sony filed against two companies who had created emulators of its PlayStation. Connectix created a PS emulator for Mac, and Bleem! did the same for Windows. Both companies *sold* their emulators, and both were forced to bow down before Sony. Connectix lost the case and Bleem! subsequently went out of business due to the legal costs (though a demo version of Bleem!'s software can still be downloaded for free online). There's also a similar 2003 case where Nintendo won a suit against a company selling a product that allowed gamers to make ROM copies of Game Boy titles to a PC. Now Game Boy might be a relic, but the fact that the company made money with the product irked Nintendo (on a side note, Nintendo has also successfully brought copyright notices against many sites that host Nintendo game ROMs, resulting in their takedowns). These cases marked the end of commercial emulators and related products, driving all similar projects to the freeware world. Come to think of it, at the end not only Nintendo, Sony, and the other game devs benefitted, but the gamers too!

Okay, I get the copyright stuff. Now how do I start playing?

As we talked about, there are two pieces of software you need to start emulating — the emulator, and the ROM. Of course, you need a decent PC to load these into, and take note that different emulators require different hardware requirements. The more recent the system that you're trying to emulate is, the more power is needed to run it.

While we're on the subject of hardware, it's also nice to have a controller that will go along with your emulator. Because PCs are so flexible, it is possible to configure the authentic controllers for each console and have them connected to their emulators. That takes manual setup for each controller and each emulator, though, so it's not for the faint of heart. For the next chapter we will take a deep dive into the world of input devices and controllers, so stay tuned.

The Best Emulators for Each System

RetroArch. This is the one emulator to rule them all, and in the eyes of many *is* the best emulator for each system. Unlike the others on this list, RetroArch breaks away from the traditional concept of emulating by being a shell or front-end for many different components or "cores". Each of these cores is meant to emulate a specific system, and each can be downloaded into RetroArch so the software can support more consoles. It's more of a hub than a traditional emulator, and that's what makes it so convenient.

Aside from powerful configurability that allows it to emulate just about any system out there, RetroArch also offers a lot of other useful functions. Its interface allows you to organize all your game files, much like a traditional game launcher. Simply save all your ROMs in a folder, then go to **Settings > Directory > File Browser Dir.** Point this to the folder where your ROMs are, and you're good to go.

Its flexibility also allows you to use any input device as a one-size-fits-all solution, letting you use your favorite controller across all your games. And if you want to really get into the retro groove, you can navigate RetroArch's interface without having to use a keyboard and mouse — its UI is very controller-friendly, so you can actually set it up in your living room TV and pretend you're back in the NES days. Most controllers that support XInput (like that of Xbox) also work out of the box without the need for any config. If you don't want to go that far and are happy with your keyboard, you can use the arrow keys to navigate instead. The X button takes the place of the traditional A button in controllers, while Z takes the place of the B button.

Of course, no system is perfect so there's a catch — the first few times working it may not exactly be a breeze. The flexibility makes the initial setup intimidating for beginners. The core system that RetroArch uses is also still a few steps away from perfection. While finding and downloading cores is easy inside the RetroArch interface (just go to **Online Updater > Core Updater**), some cores are a little harder to install than others because they have different setup steps. There are also several cores available for each system, and sometimes it's difficult to choose which is best. To save you from the trial-and-error, here are some of the best RetroArch cores you can try out first:

- Nestopia UE (for NES)
- SNES-mercury (for SNES)
- Mupen64Plus (for N64)
- DeSmuME (for DS)
- Genesis X Plus (for Sega)

RetroArch really shines in emulating older systems, and while newer consoles are also supported the cores associated with them are often plagued with compatibility issues. Hence if the game you're playing doesn't work well with a RetroArch core, and you've tried all related cores, I recommend trying a standalone emulator instead. It's also worth noting that some standalone emulators also develop RetroArch cores, though updates are shaky at best.

Despite its flaws, RetroArch is a great entry point for those looking to emulate some of the best games of their childhood. You can download RetroArch through their website.

HOME CONSOLES

FCEUX (for NES). This a standalone player for the game system that spawned some of the best franchises we know today. Have you ever wanted to play the original *Final Fantasy, Legend of Zelda,* or *Mega Man*? Then this NES emulator should do the trick.

Because the NES is such an old system, it's now much easier to create a near-perfect emulator for it. The FCEUX emulator is a striking demonstration. Offering unparalleled ease and performance, loading a game is as simple as hitting Ctrl+O and pointing the file browser towards your ROM's zip file — no unzipping is needed.

While easy to use, FCEUX also offers advanced features for those who want to up their gaming experience. You can record your session (retro streaming, anyone?) and even fiddle with some tools for a speedrun. If you want to slice and dice the ROM's performance, there are also debugging tools built-in.

The FCEUX is available for multiple platforms, and you can download the official Windows version from its website.

RetroArch Alternative - As mentioned earlier, RetroArch also supports the NES with its Nestopia UE core. Despite being an unofficial product (UE stands for "Undead Edition", the community continuation of the now-dead Nestopia core), it works like a charm despite not having all of the bells and whistles of FCEUX. In case you want something a little more alive (or if Nestopia UE doesn't work for you) then you can try the Mesen core instead.

Kega Fusion (Sega Consoles, except Dreamcast and Saturn). Sega has a catalog of gaming products that ranged from the really good to the really weird. Those seeking to experience the roller coaster of Sega's releases on the original console can look to Kega Fusion for a faithful reproduction. While it's sad that the emulator doesn't work on Dreamcast and Saturn — both consoles with a cult following and niche hits — it can run almost any game from the Genesis, Sega CD, and Game Gear catalog along with related entries.

The emulator is advanced enough to offer everything from audio and video recording, save states, online multiplayer, and more. There are also various filters (shaders) and the ability to upscale the pixely graphics. The only real weak point of this emulator is its sound since even modern technology can't perfectly emulate the unique Yamaha sound chip embedded into the original consoles.

You can download Kega Fusion <u>from its official website</u>.

RetroArch Alternative - Because Sega's consoles are made using pretty much the same system architecture, the RetroArch core Genesis X Plus is also able to emulate a wide variety of the company's consoles including the Genesis, Game Gear, Sega CD (and Mega CD), SG-1000, and the Master System. It is also a great emulator with solid support for almost all titles. It also supports BIOS files.

Wait... how about Dreamcast? Unfortunately, there really isn't a reliable emulator for Dreamcast on Windows. This is a shame since Sega's swan song console has a lot of exclusive titles that went on to become classics. Most of the Dreamcast emulation development has moved to Android, such as the ReiCast emulator (and its equivalent core for the Android RetroArch).

If you really want to try, there's DEMUL and nullDC, though both emulators are plagued by bugs and not many games are supported.

SNES9X (for SNES and Super Famicom). What's with these emulators for older consoles and the letter "X"? Well, it doesn't really matter if all you're after is playing the original release of *Chrono Trigger*. Like the FCEUX, the

SNES9X offers a lot of advanced features right under its more user-friendly ones.

Aside from doing a buttery-smooth job of emulating SNES and Super Famicom games, SNES9X also offers visual goodies such as filters and upscaling. You can even load up the online multiplayer tool and feel how the early days of multiplayer were like. If you're stuck in a particularly slow part of the game, there's a Turbo Mode that fast-forwards everything (including your progress).

You can download SNES9X from its official website.

RetroArch Alternative - Interestingly, SNES9X also creates a core for RetroArch. You can try that out if you so wish, but the definitive RetroArch core for the SNES is still bsnes-mercury. Unlike SNES9X, bsnes-mercury features more advanced settings including one that also allows the use of BIOS files in your emulation. One drawback of bsnes-mercury, however, is the fact that its minimum system requirements are a little higher than that of its peers.

Project 64 (Nintendo 64). Here is a well-loved emulator for a well-loved system. The N64 is a pretty complicated system, for its time, but Project 64 does a pretty good job of emulating it. Its fans love the simplicity, though the more advanced gamers may bemoan the lack of the fiddly bits that characterized the earlier entries in this list. It still has multiplayer, though, and it has a tool that allows you to change the game's aspect ratio. This is actually more complicated than its sounds since Project 64 does not just stretch or crop the game to fit your monitor shape. Instead, it does the change at a lower level, giving you a better experience if you have a good monitor.

One caveat, though, is that Project 64 works best with some mid-level RAM and graphics cards. The N64 marks the start of gaming consoles starting to get high-tech, and that reflects in how it is emulated. If you have a low-level machine, Project 64 may not run as smoothly as intended.

You can download the Project 64 emulator <u>from its official page</u>.

RetroArch Alternative - The mupen64plus is the absolute best RetroArch core for N64 because it is the only one such. What's good, though, is that mupen64plus is pretty much on the same level as Project 64 even in terms of plugins. The makers of mupen64plus have also created an equivalent standalone emulator for various operating systems, including Android!

Dolphin (GameCube and Wii). These two consoles may be separated by five years, but they are bound by two things. One is that they both sparked a revolution in terms of technology (at least for Nintendo), with GameCube being the first to use mini discs while the Wii being the first to use motion controls (the WiiMote and "nunchuck"). Second, they share the same system architecture that allowed a single emulator like Dolphin to stand in for both of them.

Likewise, Dolphin marks a revolution in terms of emulator technology, being the definitive crown jewel of the emulator scene. It not only performs like the original consoles — in some respects, its performance even *exceeds* its originals. Of course, it comes with a price, since Dolphin can only be run with powerful hardware. It also has a more complicated setup system than its peers on this list.

If you have the requisite horsepower and you didn't get lost during setup, you would want to give Dolphin a try. The software is chock-full of features, from basic graphic tweaks such as HD display and anti-aliasing to improvements in gameplay and controller setup. The open-source nature means you will be getting updates from the combined efforts of around 200 people who have since contributed to the project in different capacities.

It's interesting to note that Dolphin's life began *within* the lifecycle of the Wii console, meaning back while the Wii was still being sold gamers could already play its titles in HD even when the console itself can't. Now you can test this out by downloading Dolphin on its official website.

RetroArch Alternative - Well, Dolphin is so good that it doesn't need an alternative for RetroArch! The team that makes it has also produced a RetroArch core for easy download. You can expect the development to be slower on the RetroArch product than the standalone, though, so updates in the latter don't always make it to the core fast enough. Still, the cross-platform compatibility is good — you can continue your game (not literally, there's no cloud-save) on Android after you're done on the PC.

CEMU (for Wii U). Also one of the newer systems (released just a year after 3DS), the Wii U emulators are still very much works in progress. But oh boy, what a fast pace that progress is. In just a span of months, Wii U games went from absolutely unplayable to passably workable on more robust computers.

And when we say "robust", we mean a real gaming-optimized (read: i5 or higher) setup. If you're starting out with your hardware, then Wii U emulation is definitely not for you. But if you have a beefed-up rig, then go ahead and try CEMU for a round of *Mario Kart 8*.

Being under heavy development also means there are lots of hoops to jump through just to get this going, however. The devs are more concerned about which titles would work, rather than making the installation and setup painless. Because of that, expect a lot of fiddling with settings upon setup. Expect to find the latest updates locked behind a paywall too, since the devs use their Patreon accounts to get more funding for the project. Whether or not that's legal is an entirely different question, since when CEMU started Wii U's sales haven't fizzled out yet. Whatever it is, this funding scheme allows CEMU to evolve at a much faster rate than any other emulator in history.

If you have the processing power, it might be worth it to see some of your games running on vastly improved graphics on CEMU. We're talking FPS patches, anti-aliasing, 4K display, the works!

Also, don't bother looking for a RetroArch equivalent for this one. A core or two might pop up, but CEMU is really the only way to go for Wii U emulation. If you want to give it a shot, <u>you can find it at CEMU's official website</u>.

PCSX-Reloaded and PCSX2 (PSOne and PS2). The original PlayStation and its sequel PlayStation 2 weren't technically the best entrants of its generation, and yet both became immortalized as the wild-selling franchise-starters for Sony's uber-famous console line that, unlike Sega's, continue to this day. They are also remembered for bringing the world of gaming into a more mature audience, targeting the older audience largely ignored by its Sega and Nintendo rivals.

In the emulation scene, these two consoles also mark the start of terra incognita. There are no perfect emulators for both, but PCSX-Reloaded and PCSX2 come the closest. It is notable that there are thousands of titles produced for this pair of consoles alone, so the emulator devs have their work cut out for them trying to make all of them compatible. Time and again you will see a title that won't load properly, but this isn't that common.

The PCSX-Reloaded has an added complication where it requires an official PlayStation BIOS in order to run. Unfortunately, this firmware is covered by copyright, and is technically illegal to distribute — though that does not stop people from dumping it online anyway. The PCSX-Reloaded emulator may still work with low-end hardware, but you need something a little beefier if you want to emulate smoothly.

On the other hand, the PCSX 2 (built by the same team who developed the original PCSX) is a little more advanced if not a little more complicated to set up. The PS2 has multiple cores, and PCSX2 has the difficult job of emulating that. You still need a BIOS file and additional plugins in order to make everything work, but once you get everything running, loading ISOs is just a breeze. Unfortunately, the configuration itself takes a little trial and error if you want to customize your experience. Like its sibling for the PSOne, the PCSX2 is best experienced with better RAM and graphics.

You can download the PCSX-Reloaded from its official website, and the PCSX2 from its own page.

RetroArch Alternative - For PSOne, the PCSX-Reloaded devs have created a similar core called PCSX-Rearmed (see the relation?). It has pretty much the same requirements as its standalone counterpart. It's one of the pioneers in the field of RetroArch PSOne emulation, but development has been dormant for some time. While it will still work, you might fare better with more modern emulators such as Beetle PSX — a fork of another reliable (if not a tad slow) emulator Mednafen PSX — and the independently-made DuckStation.

For PS2, however, you're out of luck — there's no RetroArch core that can do what PCSX2 can do, so a standalone emulator is the only way to go.

RPCS3 (for PS3). There was some time ago when emulating the PS3 was considered impossible. The console used a weird Cell architecture that was different from its predecessors. This architecture was made to give the PS3 much greater processing power than the PSOne and PS2, but it had a major drawback — it was difficult to code for. That also meant it was incredibly difficult to emulate, so much that nobody thought of getting serious about the task.

Then RPCS3 was born and blew all contentions out of the water. While still in early (and rapid) development, the software has shown promise by allowing some titles to be fully playable — albeit, only for those with really powerful PCs. Have you tried *Demon's Souls* in 4k? It's one of the few games the emulator can run flawlessly, and it's absolutely worth it.

While it's not something you would use on a daily basis, RPCS3 is something you should definitely try if your rig can handle it. For this, <u>check out their official page for the download</u>.

As with most of the newer consoles, though, there isn't any RetroArch alternative for the PS3... yet.

HANDHELD CONSOLES

VBA-M (GameBoy series). Now we're moving into the realm of handheld consoles, which had their own fair share of classic titles and memorable gameplay. The first handheld consoles were little more than one-hit wonders, but things started picking up with the advent of GameBoy Classic — Nintendo's first foray into handhelds, and the one that let it carve out its own niche in consoles. The 8-bit GameBoy Classic evolved into the GameBoy Color and GameBoy Advance, all of which used the same architectures.

Because the GameBoys are pretty simple machines, there are lots of emulators floating around for them. There is, however, none better than VBA-M. It is a product of multiple projects merged into one (much like FCEUX) and features the ability to play both grayscale and color games. There are also graphic filters and even the ability to screenshot your gameplay. There's also a tool that allows you to fast-forward slower games, as well as one that supports auto-fire.

The only other requirement to run VBA-M is the latest version of Microsoft Direct X. Once you have that, you can run the emulator after downloading it from their website.

RetroArch Alternative - Really, there's none better than VBA-M — which is why it's also available as a RetroArch core. The system is simple enough that there is feature parity between the standalone emulator and its RetroArch sibling.

No$GBA (for DS and DSi). Nintendo pushed the boundaries of the handheld console with the dual-screen greatness on the DS and the DSi. With a massive game library, it would simply be a sin if there was no good emulator for this device.

But there is, and No$GBA (pronounced as "no-cash-GBA") is ahead of the pack. Don't be misled by its name, as the project began its life as a GameBoy Advance emulator. Today, it is one of the only few that supports both DS and DSi. It has also evolved into the fastest DS emulator, which is not an easy technical feat considering the original console had two separate processors to handle two separate screens.

Sadly, even the best has limitations. The emulator does not allow for multiplayer access, and there are also some games that won't work properly. If the latter happens to you, you can simply try another title as the supported games far outnumber the broken ones.

If you're wondering how the dual-screen process works on your PC, the second screen is operated by mouse gestures that take the place of touch controls in the original console. No$GBA also features a setting that allows you to play sideways games just as you would with the original DS. For those looking to get their hands dirty, there's also a debug tool available. You can experiment with the features No$GBA has in store by downloading it from the project's website.

RetroArch Alternative - If you already have RetroArch installed, you might want to try DeSmuME first. It's not as powerful as its standalone rival, especially with regards to its DSi compatibility. Also, DeSmuME does not support BIOS files. Despite this, most DS titles are still supported well enough for unobstructed playability. As a plus, it has a few good audio and visual options. It's pretty painless to set up, too. And since there are still similarities between the

103

Nintendo DS and the GameBoy Advance, you can even use DeSmuME to play GBA titles.

PPSSPP (PSP). As if the name itself isn't a dead giveaway. The PSP has been around for quite some time now, being Sony's answer to the DS. Featuring a wide range of features from an analog stick to web and media browsing capabilities, the PSP made a mark as one of the most iconic consoles of its generation. It helps that there's a lot of good franchises that jumped to the PSP too, such as *Tekken*, *God of War*, and *Final Fantasy*.

The age of the device made emulating it a little easier, as showcased by the top-tier PSP emulator, PPSSPP. In fact, it's really the only PSP emulator worth talking about. Optimized for PC use, the emulator can boost game graphics to about twice their original resolution, making playing on a bigger screen a visual treat. The program can even improve the resolution on some textures, making up for the low-resolution screen that was one of the original console's only weaknesses.

What's even better for those just starting out is the fact that PPSSPP needs no BIOS download to set up — which is surprising, considering emulators from the older PSOne and PS2 units need one. The PPSSPP is also packaged into an Android app, for those looking to relive the handheld nostalgia with a device they already own. Since you're on the PC, you might as well download PPSSPP <u>on its official page</u>.

Citra (for 3DS). The 3DS is one of the most modern handheld consoles, being released within the far end of the last decade. That did not stop enterprising programmer-gamers to make emulators from its code, though. But because of the modern system and the hobbyist nature of many of these emulators, they're not as mature as some of the entries we've had earlier. They're not recommended for real-world gaming, but you can still give them a shot if you feel so inclined.

Among the 3DS emulators that have sprung up, Citra is easily the best. It's been through a rapid development phase, which has given it a lot of great features. It's still very much a work in progress though, so expect several bugs along the way (including but not limited to sound errors and slow games). Controller setup could also use a little more work, as analog sticks don't work right out of the box.

Citra generally allows for painless initial configuration, but you will find that some games — especially Pokemon titles — will require a lot of additional work. And because the 3DS has a few extra features such as the gyroscope (not inherently supported on PC) some titles that make heavy use of them will not work properly. Still, if you want to check out how *Ocarina of Time* or *Kingdom Hearts* fared during their 3D incarnations, they'll run just fine.

Unfortunately, there's no good RetroArch core to recommend for this or any of the newer systems, so if you want to try out 3DS gaming you'd better stick with standalone programs. For that, <u>head over to the official website to download Citra</u>.

Yuzu (for Nintendo Switch). As if creating a dual-screen handheld console wasn't enough, Nintendo topped its own ingenuity again with the advent of the Switch. With its groundbreaking technology and a complementary list of awesome games, it's *the* console to get if you're into portable gaming. Unless you're part of the PC Master Race and you have a laptop.

The emulator for the Switch stands with RPCS3 on the cutting edge of the emulator community, as one of the newest consoles to have a working emulator. Yuzu comes from the same development team as Citra, endowing it with the same brisk development pace. At most, you have games that are *almost* completely playable, but at least most of the important features are there. You can try a round of *Super Smash Bros. Ultimate*, and while it's got the fun down pat, there are some significant bugs. You can try *Shovel Knight* with very few issues, though, so there's that.

Perhaps an even bigger issue than making games work is getting the game ROMs themselves without resorting to outright piracy. Since the Switch is still very new, Nintendo maintains it in active development. New titles are still being released, and Nintendo is also actively cracking down on websites that host the ROMs of games still in circulation.

Just as for the more modern handheld consoles here, RetroArch does not have a good answer to the standalone effort that is Yuzu. If you want to try the latest release of this emulator, <u>head over to its official site</u>.

ARCADE

MAME. Once upon a time, consoles were nothing but toys for the geeks or the obscenely rich. When the kid average Joe wants to have fun, he scrounges up a few quarters and heads to the arcade. That's not an experience the younger generation may remember fondly (thanks to the consoles being cheaper than ever, and thanks to PCs transforming into gaming behemoths), but many of us still do.

But even sadder than the short-lived golden age of arcades is the fact that many games never made it to other platforms. These games, like those of long-dead consoles, remained stuck in their colorful cabinets, awaiting rescue. For those who were able to capture these games' souls in ROMs and ISOs, there isn't really a place where they can be transferred and played again — until MAME came along.

MAME (the Multiple Arcade Machine Emulator) has the distinction of being one of the few emulators created solely for the preservation of old arcade games. Of course, that's just legalese for "this software lets you play arcade games like the old times". If you can find a ROM of your favorite classic, chances are you can load it up in MAME, go full-screen, and play like it's the late 80s. The emulator can even handle those complicated Neo-Geo games SNK made for some time, along with the CPS1/2/3 boards by Capcom. This turns your PC into a legit arcade machine! Maybe it's time to relive the glory days of the original *Metal Slug*. Or maybe you want to go even further back in time to... *Computer Space*?

While MAME hasn't received significant updates in some time, it has incrementally increased its support for various ROMs. Because of its "history-first" outlook, you can't expect any additional features such as those for debugging or improving game visuals. The good news, though, is that it comes as a RetroArch core — really putting "Retro" to the name. You can download MAME via its official webpage.

What about newer consoles?

What about the Xbox series? Or PS Vita? Or the later PS versions?

Sadly, no dice on these later consoles. As you may have noticed, the progress of emulation stops at PS3 for the home consoles and Nintendo Switch for the handhelds. Anything later and any existing emulator project will give you a mishmash of error messages and bugs — provided, of course, that you can even get into the game's loading screen.

Of course, that isn't to say that there aren't existing projects. For the PS Vita, for example, there's the **Vita3K** that aims to be the go-to emulator for the console. The problem is that there aren't any commercial games that will work with it. It's even farther off from a complete release than the RPCS3, and for now, it only supports homebrew games that some enterprising amateur devs have made. If you want to try a little homemade *VitaQuake* (no, it's not a cereal brand) then you can try this out.

As for the Xbox series, Microsoft isn't well known for its generosity when it comes to proprietary code. That has prevented many Xbox emulators from taking off, even if the first Xbox has been around for a very long time. The only real Xbox emulator to watch out for is a project called **CxBx Reloaded**, a 64-bit only software that is still in the beta stage. You can try it out from its official website, but don't expect it to work flawlessly just yet. It still needs some time to mature.

For the PS4, there is a project called **Orbital** which is still in the very early development stage — so early that the dev is still yet to completely reverse-engineer the console's code. Because of the spare-time nature of many of these projects, it may be another year before Orbital and similar projects can take you to a game's loading screen.

And as for the PS5... well, let's just it's still a pipe dream, and Sony will probably sue the living daylights of anyone who tries emulating it at this point.

"But," I hear you saying, "I Googled and there are lots of other emulators for the Xbox and PS4!" I should warn you now — be VERY careful when downloading these emulators! The reason they aren't included in this list is either because they don't work as well as our selections, or they're completely fake. Take the scammy "PCSX4", for example, that takes after the PCSX and PCSX2. It's complete with its own site and Github page, along with YouTube demos and all. But when you try to download it, the site takes you to a survey form instead. This is just one of the many scams that try to hitch a ride in the emulator hype, trying to rob unsuspecting gamers. If you're trying your luck with emulators not listed here, make sure to do your research carefully.

Watch out for surprises!

Remember, though, that technology evolves faster than you can say "emulator". As you may have noticed, a few of the emulators in this list sprang up at lightning speed, going from concept to product in just months. New solutions are being developed for problems, and new technologies are always being leveraged to help the gaming world progress.

That means you shouldn't worry if you don't have emulator access for your favorite console or game. Someday in the near future someone will be able to make THE perfect emulator, that runs all titles, on all machines. Who knows when it will drop... maybe tomorrow, maybe next week, or next month... The only thing we're sure of is that somewhere out there, a gamer is developing something magical.

Most of the emulators on our list, when they were released, were pretty much surprises. Some of them even arrived in the wake of claims that "such and such console can't be emulated!". So keep your eyes pealed for news from the workshops of the glorious PC Master Race!

The Best Places for Free ROMs

Again the warning: downloading pirated copies of copyrighted ROMs is illegal. Selling them is illegal as well, so be warned!

Now that we've got that out of the way, and now that you probably have an emulator or two installed on your PC, let's find out where you can get ROMs to match.

The easiest way to get your hands on a ROM is to find one which is either in the public domain (no longer under copyright) or one that has already been abandoned (abandonware, as when a publisher has gone out of business). The **PDRoms** website hosts thousands of ROMs from different consoles (and generations), all of them copyright-free and thus free for download by anyone. Abandonware, which is no longer distributed or supported (though technically still under inactive copyright), is collected in **MyAbandonware**. This is a great place for older classics, with thousands of ROMs in its catalog. There are even newer games here, with the most recent ones being within the previous decade. Remember that the potential existence of copyright puts these games in a legal gray area, but there's probably a higher chance of you being struck with lightning while reading this than being sued by an inactive game dev.

If you're feeling adventurous, try out "homebrew" titles such as the *VitaQuake* we mentioned earlier. These titles are edits or reproductions of gameplay from established commercial games, lovingly worked on by aspiring developers. There are scores of these collected in sites like **NESWorld** and **RomHacking**. Don't expect top-level graphics and gameplay complete with support — they may exist, but not guaranteed by the enthusiasts behind them. Don't brush them off as second-rate products either — remember that the incredibly famous *DOTA* was once upon a time just a homebrew mod of a *Warcraft* game.

"But," I hear you cry out again, "what about those big titles you mentioned earlier? Not all of them are abandoned or in the public domain!" If that's the case, then they're still copyright-protected. And that only means one thing — you need to buy them. Anything else would be breaking the law.

Though the jury is still out on its legality, many consider it a fair practice to get the ROMs of the games they already own so they could play it on PC. That means you can buy a game then extract the ROM (if you have the technical know-how) or just download it off a Google search. Thus emulation can be a workaround for those who do not have the requisite console for the game, or those in areas where the original games were not localized (but where translation patches for ROMs exist). After all, buying the game means you have already pitched with your support for the game devs, and that's all that matters.

CHAPTER 4: You're In Control!

One of the things that console gamers throw against the PC Master Race is that the latter can't "feel" the games with a keyboard and a mouse. Sometimes that's true — console experts may not pride themselves on their precision when it comes to mouse movement and shortcut keys, but there's something to be said about their lightning-quick finger reflexes and the smooth flow of their coordinated button-mashing. Indeed, some games (especially fighting games) take on a different, more intense feel on a controller. It's the opposite of how MOBAs and some shooters just aren't the same without a keyboard and mouse.

Except that whoever levies these allegations against PC gamers sorely underestimates just how versatile a PC can be. In fact, PCs can take on just about any controller you can throw at it, from the easily-compatible Xbox controllers to the Bluetooth-based Joy-Cons of the Switch. Not everything works out of the box, but this chapter is dedicated to making sure your gaming arsenal is completely in your control.

The Two APIs

To begin understanding how controllers work, let me re-introduce you to a term you most likely have heard before when browsing tech-related information.

An API (Application Programming Interface;+10 geek points!) is that thing that connects an item (in our case the controller) to the system (in our case the PC). It allows the item to "talk" to the system. Without an API, plugging an item into a system would be like plugging in an appliance to a dead outlet.

There are two primary APIs used in allowing controllers to "talk" to PCs. First is theXInput API, and the second is the DirectInput API. You need to know this because, for the most part, it is XInput compatibility that we are looking for when looking for a controller. This is the newer, and better-supported API that many modern consoles use. Naturally, this is also the API that is supported by PCs out of the box. The perfect example of this is the Xbox controller, which works perfectly from the get-go because PCs are programmed to immediately understand its XInput system. So that's your first tip — if you have an Xbox controller lying around (or you can get one on the cheap) you're good to go for controller gaming. Xbox controllers work well with almost any type of game you want to play!

Of course, Windows is all about choice and you have the option to use pretty much any other console you want. Partial to PSOne controllers, maybe? Can't blame you, those ones are nostalgic. Older controllers use DirectInput API, and in order to use them, you will have to do some additional configuration. There are tools that work as a go-between to help your PC understand DirectInput as if it was XInput. These XInput emulators can come in handy, though there are some limitations.

For the rest of this chapter, I'll lead you through every kind of console controller on the market (and then some) and tell you how you can attach those to your PC!

Choose Your Weapon

Xbox Controllers (One and 360). These are considered the ideal PC gaming controllers because of their availability, compatibility, and simplicity of use. You can literally just take one and plug it in, and you're good to go! In some instances, you will have to wait until your PC downloads the appropriate drivers, but these updates happen automatically so you don't have to manually intervene.

You can also connect your controller wirelessly via Bluetooth. How easy this is will depend on whether Bluetooth is a built-in function of both the controller and the PC you are using. Newer controllers (Xbox One) have Bluetooth as one of their features, so you can just access the connectivity setting in your PC to pair them. You can do this by searching for **Settings** in the Start menu, then going to **Devices > Bluetooth**. If you have an Xbox Wireless dongle, you can pair your controller by going to the above option, then clicking **Add Bluetooth or other device**. From here, go to **Everything else** then **Xbox Wireless Controller**. If your controller does not support Bluetooth (but it can support wireless), you can also buy one of these dongles and do the same steps to set it up.

What's also great with having a modern Xbox controller is that you'll have the option of updating your controller's firmware straight from your PC (Windows 10 only). Like other devices, controllers have their own programming that can be improved by future updates. Microsoft regularly releases these firmware updates to resolve controller bugs. For this, you need to download the **Xbox Accessories** app from the Windows Store (you can find this by searching, or as an icon on your taskbar). Long-press the connected controller, and you will see an "Update Required" prompt on the Accessories app screen if a firmware update is available (if not, "Device Info" and "Configure" will appear instead). Click on the prompt, and your controller will receive the new firmware in the next few moments.

Aside from all these conveniences, there are other reasons why the modern Xbox controllers top the rest of what's available in the market. They are very ergonomic, and the traditional 4-way D-pad improves accuracy (compared to the disc-like pad of earlier versions). The shoulder buttons are located exactly where the fingers land and are just as snappy and responsive as the other buttons on this solid controller. The feedback also extends to the triggers, for more immersive gameplay.

PlayStation 4. If your previous trips to the backwaters of console gaming have left you enamored with the sleeker designs of PS controllers, don't fret. Windows also play nice with PS4 controllers, and you can use one without much fuss.

Like with Xbox controllers, you can simply plug your PS4 controller into any Windows 10 device and it will work without any fiddling. For wireless, you would need a separate DualShock 4 wireless adapter with which to play.

The major limitation with PlayStation 4 is that if you're using a game without innate DualShock 4 support — which is still a lot of games out there — you need to independently configure your controller with the game launcher you are using. If you're playing on Steam, for example, you need to go into Steam's **Settings** (under **Big Picture Mode**) and go to **Controller Settings > PS4 Controller Support**. From here you can check out other settings such as light bar color and stick sensitivity. You can also remap buttons and change many other options, perfect for those who want to fully customize the gaming experience.

Like the Xbox One controller, the PS4 controller is also a great improvement over its predecessors. It's more ergonomic, and there are also input improvements such as the addition of a touchpad and the shooter-friendly gyroscope.

PlayStation 3. While latest-generation controllers like the two previously mentioned can be easily set up on the PC, PS3 and older controllers will require a bit more setup. This comes in the form of new drivers you have to download.

We're talking about ScpToolkit, a nice little open-source software that allows you to modify system drivers to get the DualShock 3 controller working. You can Google the ScpToolkit GitHub page to make sure you get the latest version available. Just download the file, and go through the install process.

The installation process gives you an option on what parts of the toolkit you'd like to install, and you should click everything except for "Gamepad Analyzer" and "Debug Info Collector" (nothing wrong if you install them, though). Once the kit is installed, you'll be asked to run the driver installer, and doing so should show you options for your (connected) PS3 controller.

Once you're on this page, click on **Initialize All Connected Devices**, and wait until the required drivers are installed. Hit the **Next** button, and the next process (more drivers and controller recognition) will start.

Up next is an option that you **MUST SKIP**. That is unless you have a spare Bluetooth dongle you're not using, which you're willing to pair permanently to your PS3 controller. You would be apprised of this danger by the huge WARNING sign on that page. Basically, installing wireless in this step converts the attached dongle to be your permanently-dedicated PS3 controller receiver. If you install it on the wrong dongle (like, say, a keyboard or mouse receiver) then you're up for a headache. If you ever decide to push with a wireless connection, make sure your desired dongle is the only one plugged in before hitting Initialize All Connected Devices. If you'd like to skip it, just hit **Next**.

Second to the last in the process is allowing your DualShock 3 to control on-screen movement by tricking your computer to think that it's an Xbox 360 controller. Windows is pretty territorial, you see, and it tends to turn a cold shoulder to old controllers not made by Microsoft. Installing the Xbox 360 driver allows you to expand the compatibility of your controller to even more games.

Finally, there's a Windows Service that allows the OS to better communicate with the controller. After this, you're done! Thanks to the Xbox 360 drivers, any Windows game that supports Xbox controllers (which is virtually every game) will now work with your PS3 controller.

PlayStation 1 and PlayStation 2. These are probably the consoles that let you experience your first stretch of in-home gaming back in the days, and nostalgia is a legit reason for having used them. That said, they follow the same setup instructions as PS3 controllers plus one important caveat.

PS1 and PS2 controllers do not use USB, so there's no way to plug them in directly to the PC. They don't support wireless either, so your only option is to purchase a PS-to-USB adapter. These are available online, though not always in-stock. If you're buying a controller anyway, it's best to shoot above these controllers and go for a PS3 or later instead.

Xbox (First Generation). Another nostalgic gaming device, but considering it's also from Microsoft it's confusing why set up isn't easy. It's doable, but a far cry from the plug-and-play convenience of its successors.

First, you would need an adapter as you would with a PS 1 or 2. There are also Xbox-to-USB adapters available online. Next, you would need to download an archive called XBCD that allows your PC to recognize the controller. The XBCD archive contains a diver, a couple of auxiliary folders and files, and the .exe installer itself. Run the installer once downloaded, and depending on whether you're using a 32-bit or 64-bit Windows OS.

For 32-bit Windows users, the setup is pretty much on rails and you just have to click-through to finish it. In the end, your PC should recognize your controller's inputs. However, 64-bit users may encounter a weird error message. This is where things start to get tricky.

The error message is typically caused by an integrity check that 64-bit Windows does on the installation. The XBCD project is open-source freeware, meaning it does not raise funds to buy the online certificates (which costs hundreds of dollars) needed to get the software to pass Windows' scrutiny.

As a workaround, you can disable integrity checking instead to allow the setup to proceed. This is done by double-clicking the **disable.bat** file that is found inside the XBCD folder. After this, reboot the PC and retry the installation process.

Hopefully, this will get you up and working, but if it doesn't you can check out the XBCD help docs. The extensive documentation provides you with descriptions of potential problems, along with their resolutions. Surprisingly, there's a lot that could possibly go wrong while installing on a 64-bit device, and you might have to go into the PC's Start-up Settings just to fix it.

Once you're through with everything, the XBCD project also includes a tool that allows you to test and calibrate your controller. Simply pull up a Run dialog (WinKey + R) and type **joy.cpl**. Click on the Test tab on the upper-right, and you could check how the buttons respond.

In the interest of time (and potentially your sanity), I recommend just buying a more modern controller if you don't have one yet. Still, if you have a first-generation Xbox controller lying around and collecting dust, it's nice to know that there's a way to make it work.

Nintendo Switch (Joy-Con, Pro). Speaking of modern controllers, the ultra-portable Joy-Con and the Xbox-like Pro controller from Nintendo's hybrid console also work surprisingly well. Once connected via Bluetooth, they work perfectly. Just go to **Settings** then click on **Devices > Bluetooth**. From here, you can add a Bluetooth device.

For the Joy-Con, once you're done with the Bluetooth sync in the PC, long-press the **Sync** button at the top of the Pro controller, beside the charging port. The Sync is between the SL and SR buttons. The long-press will put the controller in pairing mode, after which it will appear in the Bluetooth menu on your PC. Select it, and you're off!

It is possible to pair both Joy-Cons, or more than one controller when doing multiplayer. As of now, however, you can't join both Joy-Cons as a single controller. The only issue you will encounter is that Switch's controllers still use the old DirectInput API instead of XInput, so you might have compatibility issues with some games. For this, you can use a program (just like with the other controllers) to make your PC think that your Switch controller is an Xbox controller. For starters, you can try downloading the latest release of x360ce from GitHub. Once paired, you can also toggle sensitivity and other controller settings in your game launcher if supported.

The Switch Pro controller takes things up a notch, sporting instant connectivity out of the box just like the DualShock 4... as long as you're on Steam. The platform natively emulates XInput for hassle-free pairing and gaming. If you're not on Steam, follow the instructions to get an XInput emulator above.

Joy-Cons and Switch Pro controllers are great for their tech, sporting gyro aiming and motion control. They also have NFC built-in, allowing you to interact with other NFC-enabled items for your games.

Wii (Remotes and U Pro Controllers). Just as with the Switch, Nintendo's Wii and Wii U Pro controllers will pair effortlessly with Windows through the same Bluetooth settings as above.

However, support for actual gaming input will depend on the emulator you are using. Dolphin, the definitive emulator for Wii and Wii U, supports these controllers though some games may have glitches. Still, if you're playing mainstream titles, support should be stable enough.

GameCube (And WaveBird). I guess this console controller is the best example of why Nintendo's Windows compatibility is simply astonishing. All you have to do is get an adapter that allows you to plug it into a USB port, and it will work as intended! What's more, Nintendo also has its own official adapter, originally made to allow GameCube controllers to work with the Wii U for a 4-way game of *Super Smash Bros.* There are also third-party adapters that allow you to do the same. It's even better if you use the controller with Dolphin, which allows you to use the device for its Wii U emulation, therefore reducing the occurrence of any potential bugs.

SNES. Did I mention my marvel at Nintendo's Windows compatibility earlier? I really should have saved that for this one. The old SNES controllers might not be the best to use for long stretches of gaming, they are still plug-and-play compatible so long as you have an adapter. May Flash offers a really good adapter that allows you to hook up two SNES controllers, and there's also a switch for DirectInput and XInput.

Maybe SNES is a little too plain and outdated for you, but you still like its retro aesthetics? Then a third-party clone might be best for you — and we'll be discussing one a little later.

Steam Controller. Far from being a simple storefront and game launcher, Steam has also dipped its skilled fingers into hardware. This jaunt resulted in an interesting concept called the Steam Controller, an ultra-customizable controller (at least within the Steam platform) that can also do anything that your keyboard, mouse, and other controllers can do.

While the Steam Controller never gained mainstream traction, it still works, and even better it's completely Windows-compatible. Just plug it in via a micro USB cable, or use the wireless dongle that comes with the device. All the customization and remapping (you can program full keyboard shortcuts on the buttons!) can also be done via the **Big Picture Mode**, the same as you would when tweaking a PS4 controller.

Logitech F310. This is one of the best-known and best-loved third-party controllers, simply because it does everything right — so long as you don't throw it across the room while rage-quitting since it's not as solid as an original console controller.

Aside from working well with a lot of PC games, it offers a familiarity that stems largely from its PlayStation-like shape and button arrangement. Even better, it's built with a switch that allows the controller to work either in XInput Mode or DirectInput Mode. This means you can use it for a whole host of PC titles, new or old, without configuring anything.

Astro C40 TR. If the Steam Controller is too eccentric for you, and the Logitech too flimsy, you might want to break into your bank account and buy one of these premium babies. With the build quality of a tank and the combined features of some of the greatest controllers out there, the Astro C40 TR is the Maserati of third-party controllers. It is completely customizable, and has swappable components. You can even rearrange the components physically, so you can have the sticks layout of the Xbox or the PS on a whim.

What's best is that it works flawlessly on PC, and all you have to do is to plug it in. I do wish it comes with a Kensington lock though — for that price, it's not a controller you can afford to misplace.

8Bitdo SN30 Pro. Let's take a hairpin turn and move from the uber-high tech to the uber-retro in third-party controllers. The SN30 Pro is a copy of the old SNES controllers, with updates for the modern gaming world. These include dual sticks, vibration, and trigger buttons. If not for the shape, you would have mistaken it for a modern controller!

The gamepad's shape is its biggest weakness, however, since its ergonomics are very limited. Still, it's a plug-and-play affair that works not just with Windows but with a whole host of other OSes — even Android. If you want to push the limits, there's also a Pro+ model that has customizable buttons and other modern options.

Ultra-cheap, third-party controllers. Just want a controller, *any* controller? If you're not picky at all, it's possible to get one of those China-made gamepads from the Internet, at less than $5 apiece. No, seriously. Don't look down on them because they seriously work! They have none of the trappings of branded products and have the old, bland style of older PlayStation joysticks, but they have all the right buttons and a USB connection — pretty much all you need to play. As for compatibility, you might need to configure that separately. RetroArch, for example, tends to recognize the wrong controller type, but you can easily correct this by going to **Settings > Input** and pressing the corresponding buttons for the software to recognize.

Guitar Controllers and Drum Sets. A fan of *Guitar Hero*? The game has several releases across different consoles, but fans will know it's never the same unless you're playing it with a guitar controller. As a PC gamer, you should check out *CloneHero* instead. Aside from being a fun clone of the famous series, the game's documentation also has a complete list of all the guitar controllers that are supported by the game.

The same is true for almost all other games that support guitar controllers, so you need to do a little research to see if your emulator and your game works with the controller you have. If everything's in harmony, then you could just buy an adapter, plugin, and start shredding!

Driving Wheels, Light Guns, Dance Mats, Fight Sticks, Flight Controls, and more. As you would have probably noticed by now, there are two important things that will determine whether or not a controller will work with your PC. First is the hardware interface, which is whether or not you can plug your device into a USB port. The second is the software interface, which is whether or not the PC can read what's happening when a button is pushed.

More niche controllers such as wheels, guns, arcade-style fight sticks, and controllers for flight sims are almost exclusively sold by third-party manufacturers, and each will have its own compatibility specs. If they are made for PC gaming, then you can expect a plug-and-play affair regardless of the niche. If they are made for a different console, then you would need a hardware adapter at the very minimum.

It really helps if you're using a game launcher that supports a bevy of controllers like Steam does. The launcher has native support for modern controllers, along with their special features like gyro aiming. This makes shooters that much more fun and controller-related headaches that much more infrequent.

You can also check with the community behind the game you're playing what controllers they support. We've already talked about *CloneHero* with its detailed support page. Other games that have been cloned and ported, such as

GuitarFreaks, *DrumMania*, and *osu!* also have bustling communities that have created patches and expansions supporting various controllers. Usually, it's these communities that are responsible for pushing the limits of controller support, extending the standard range of games to cover even cutting-edge controllers like VR headsets.

If your controller doesn't work with your game, you might need X360CE to allow the PC to interpret its controls as that of an Xbox controller. Depending on the type of controller, you may also remap its buttons through Steam's Big Picture Mode, or through a third-party app like AntiMicro.

CHAPTER 5: Graphics — The Big Picture

Do you ever wonder why gamers obsess over graphics more than most other aspects of gaming? Hang around gamers long enough and you'd hear them talk about what graphics card and monitor they have more than what RAM and what CPUs they have... even though a computer can run just fine without a graphics card, but not without the other two.

To put it simply, most gamers are in it for the thrill of seeing an entire world (or universe) unfold with all its action, in front of their very eyes. The more realistic the visuals, the more engaging everything is. Unless you're strictly into an emulation or retro gaming, you're likely to find that sooner or later you want to see the world you're diving into in much clearer detail. After all, game devs design most games to squeeze as much juice out of your graphics card as possible, for your enjoyment.

And yeah, of course, it's bragging rights too — the king of the roost is that guy who can go on gaming long after the rest of his friends have had their PC insides turned into molten mush.

But if we're going to talk about graphics, it's not just the graphics card we must talk about. Indeed, we need to look at something much more basic, the monitor. Then we'll work towards more complicated stuff, like adjusting your game's graphics so that it works perfectly with the equipment you have.

One thing to note before we dive in — do **NOT** buy anything else yet after finishing this chapter. You might be tempted to go out and add a monitor and a graphics card to your shopping cart, but both of these share intricate relations with other parts of your PC. If you're planning on building or upgrading, at least hold on to any purchase until after you finish the next chapter so that you know how to find parts that work well with each other. It would be a shame to buy a cool GPU and find out that your power supply can't spare enough juice for it!

Monitoring the Specs

Here's something that monitor manufacturers wouldn't tell you — most of the products on the market aren't that different from each other. Most of the marketing-speak that you hear about monitors don't really translate to real-life experiences. Contrast ratios, for example, are often vastly exaggerated. Differences in latency are often too small to actually be experienced.

Despite this, there *are* important things you should know about monitors so that you could choose the best one for your gaming needs (and your budget, of course). There are two major types of monitors depending on the technology that the panel type uses. There are TFT LCD monitors, which are older and less sharp than the clearer and thinner IPS monitors. The latter, being the current crop of monitor technology, is often more expensive. Both types of monitors, though, have different specs that you need to pay attention to. These are listed below. Note that we're not going through self-explanatory specs like brightness and viewing angle, and instead we'll focus on the numbers that have the potential to impact your game.

Screen Size. First up, there's the most basic difference among all monitors — the size. The inches of the screen is measured diagonally, meaning you draw your tape measure across the screen from one corner to the opposite. Note that there isn't really a standard way of dealing with where to start the measure, so some manufacturers inflate their screen sizes by measuring from the bezel. If you can, find the **viewable size** spec since this is the one that lists the actual size of the screen.

Aspect Ratio. This is the ratio of the horizontal to the vertical size of the unit. The most common measures are 4:3, 6:9, and 16:10. 4:3 means that for every 4 inches across, there will be 3 units of a monitor's height (resulting in a TV-like shape, which characterizes older monitors). More powerful resolutions often affect the aspect ratio of monitors. For example, a 1080p (1920x1080 pixels) has a 16:9 aspect ratio, while a higher resolution of 1920x1200 pixels finds home in a 16:10 aspect ratio.

Resolution. This is another of the basic monitor specs you'll see flying around. Simply put, the higher the resolution, the more pixels are crammed into the viewable space of the monitor, and the sharper the image quality is. In a 1920x1080 resolution, 1920 refers to the number of pixels found horizontally, while 1080 is the vertical count of pixels. The higher the resolution, the better (and more expensive) the monitor is.

You've probably been hearing a lot of resolution-related specs being thrown around — 720p, 1080p, and 4K UHD. These are all basic naming conventions — 720p is 1280x720 pixels, 1080p is 1920x1080 pixels, and 4K is 3840x2160. As you would have noticed, 4K breaks the naming convention established by older standards. This is mostly for marketing as well, since it signifies that a 4K monitor can fit 4 1080p images inside it. Pretty neat, huh? Pretty expensive, too.

Especially when you consider it's no longer the latest and greatest since 8K monitors are now cropping up. There are also odd resolutions such as 1440p (Quad HD, or four times 720p) and 1800p (Quad HD+, the middle-ground between QHD and 4K).

Every other spec tends to improve the higher the resolution is, so most gamers shoot for the biggest that money can buy. In reality, though, that's not a must. Most gamers do their thing on older monitors, and they're happy with it. Only those on the bleeding edge of AAA title releases would really ache for much higher resolutions. It doesn't matter if your monitor is just 720p, as long as your game works well with it (and as long as it's configured properly for it). If you are under a budget, performance will always come first before eye-candy. Besides, it makes no sense to buy a powerful monitor if you don't have the graphics card to power its specs.

Another related stat is the **pixel pitch**, which refers to how big the gap is between the pixels. The smaller the pitch, the less chance that your eye can pick up the separation of the pixels — and the better your viewing experience will be.

Display Colors. The higher the better, as more colors mean your monitor can reproduce images as realistically as possible. The standard is currently at 16.7 million colors, but if you have an IPS panel you're probably going to have much higher numbers.

Contrast Ratio. In technical terms, this is the number of shades that the screen can produce between the darkest black and the brightest white. However, many manufacturers confound it with techno-babble such as DCF, DCR, ASCR, and ACM. If you want to find the real contrast ratio, search for "native contrast ratio" (usually listed at the end). The common benchmark is 1000:1. The higher the first number, the better the monitor's contrast ratio really is. Dynamic ratios are often just false indicators.

Refresh Rate. Here's one of the monitor specs that gamers obsess about. Think of monitors as an array of light bulbs (pixels) that change color every so often in order to create the illusion of a moving image. The refresh rate is the measure of how often this change occurs. The higher the refresh rate (measured in Hertz or Hz) the faster the screen can display changes. Some games, such as shooters and MOBAs, can depend greatly on refresh rate to accurately show you what's happening around you.

Of course, monitors that have higher refresh rates are more expensive. Currently, 240Hz is the upper practical limit, but you'll more commonly find monitors with 60Hz and 120Hz refresh rates. The former is more familiar for daily use, but the latter is the one preferred by serious gamers since they play best with 3D scenes.

There's also an interesting relationship between refresh rate and resolution. If you had the money, you would go for a 4K monitor that goes up to 144Hz (the esports standard) right? Unfortunately, you can't. This is a technical limitation imposed by the cables through which the signals from the CPU (or GPU) to the monitor pass through. Every aspect of the monitor — resolution, color, refresh rate — takes up a piece of the bandwidth, and what the market offers can't deliver on all these specs when jacked up to 11. If you're gaming and you need to be as agile as possible, doing 144Hz on a QHD+ monitor would be best. If you're just out to admire the colorful open world of your game, then you can sacrifice the refresh rate for a 4K monitor on 10-bit color.

Related to the refresh rate is another stat called **Response Time**. This isn't a reliable indicator of performance, since manufacturers measure it differently. Usually, it's how fast a pixel changes from black, to white, and to black again. Some, however, measure it as how fast the pixel changes from gray to black (or white) and back to gray. This could really skew the numbers, hence why some manufacturers tend to flaunt their product's response times. Gray-to-gray measurement is inherently faster than black-to-white-to-black, so beware when making a purchase.

Graphic Differences

Aside from the monitor, the graphics card is the only other thing that could bring you the visual satisfaction that the latest games aim to deliver (okay, maybe not the *only one*, but you get the idea). Graphic cards — also called GPUs or Graphical Processing Units — also enjoy a close relationship with monitors. Basically, if you have a high-level monitor, you need a high-level graphics card (and vice versa) to bring out the best of each other. If you don't have a high-spec monitor, you may not even need a graphics card and vice versa. Of course, however, you will only need high-specs on either if you are actually playing games that require them!

Just like monitors, there are LOTS of graphic cards out there. However, they often fall into two camps: Nvidia and AMD. Soon, Intel might join the fray as it preps to roll out its Xe graphics. But until that happens, gamers are divided into either "Team Green" or "Team Red".

As it did in its CPU segment, AMD has grown by leaps and bounds over the past few years. It has released its top-of-the-line RX 6000 cards, rivaling the GeForce RTX 3080 flagship from Nvidia's side of the turf. Both camps are also competing on the software side, with Team Green flaunting its DLSS 2.0 which provides an AI-assisted boost for your resolution. This significantly ups your PC's performance with as few compromises as possible. While relatively few games support DLSS as of now, it's something you'd want to keep an eye on. Team Red, on the other hand, has its own Fidelity FX Super Resolution which aims to do the same. Unfortunately, AMD's open-source answer to the DLSS isn't quite ready for prime time yet, as a v.1.0 release has not yet been made as of the time of this writing.

Both manufacturers also straddle all segments of the GPU industry, producing everything from ultra-cheap to ultra-expensive cards. We're talking about sub-$100 to sub $2,000 GPUs here! If you're gaming and you've decided you need a graphics card (i.e., your CPU does not have integrated graphics), steer clear of the lowest tier and shoot for at least the mid or lower-mid.

"But," I head you ask once more, "what's the mid or lower-mid when it comes to GPUs?" Hold your horses — the answer lies in the following specs.

Memory Amount. This is the most important spec in a GPU. The more the merrier, but if you're starting out then a card with a 6GB memory would set you up just fine for basic gaming. If you're planning to go full 1080p with your games, then an 8GB card should be good.

Ports. This is also very important, as you need to make sure that your GPU supports the monitor you have. There are various ports available, such as HDMI, DisplayPort, DVI, VGA, and USB-C. If you buy the wrong card (or monitor), you'd need to buy a separate adapter. And don't get started on which port is best for gaming — it's just a race between

HDMI and DisplayPort, but as each release trumps the latest of the other party, it's really an endless discussion.

Dimensions. This seems like a no-brainer, but it's still not the first thing you would check. Each motherboard has expansion slots for graphic cards, but some graphic cards occupy more space than what common sense dictates. Aside from varying in height, length, and thickness, some cards occupy two and even three slots at once!

For gaming, most cards are full-height (as opposed to the slim or half-height form factor) and eat up two slots. As some unwritten rule, the newer the card, the bulkier it is. We're not even talking about fan shrouds and heatsinks, which take up additional space in your case. Look for a card that physically fits with the rig you have now (or plan to have).

Thermal Design Power. Appearing as TDP on the spec sheet, this is a double-purpose number that primarily measures heat dissipation, and also gives an idea of how many watts are needed to fire up the GPU. You might see a different number on Nvidia called Total Graphics Power (TGP), but that's the same concept in a different measure. Miles and kilometers, basically.

This number on its own doesn't mean anything, but if you take into account your CPU and your power supply you'll get a picture of whether your parts will complement each other. For example, a 400-watt power supply will have difficulty running a 250-watt graphics card and a 95-watt CPU. Remember, other components are also consuming their own share of power. If this is the case you'd need to upgrade to a 600-watt power supply to be on the safe side.

There are several wattage calculators available online to help you measure how your parts would work with each other, so take advantage of those before committing to a purchase.

Power Connectors. The PCIe slot of your motherboard gives out a maximum of 75W, which is far south of what any decent GPU would need. This is why graphics cards always need supplemental power connectors. These come in either 6-pin or 8-pin (or 12-pin, though they have 8-pin adaptors), and there are cards that don't come in both. It's important to make sure that your power supply has the same supplemental connectors needed for the graphics card, else you'll have to buy a new one. You're able to draw power from Molex or SATA connectors, but these adapters aren't meant for long-term use.

GFLOPS/TFLOPS. These are two terms used to measure the maximum performance a GPU can dish out. GFLOPS stands for "billions of floating-point operations per second" (where G means Giga, as in gigabytes = a billion bytes) and TFLOPS stands for "trillions of floating-point operations per second". With this measure, you can compare two GPUs of the same architecture to find out which is faster than the other. The higher the number is, the better the graphics card performs.

Clock Speed. Unlike in CPUs, clock speed isn't as important for a graphics card. For one, these numbers can get pretty skewed due to the effects of other GPU specs. For example, a GPU with a high clock speed buy with an older architecture could perform less in the real world than one with a lower clock speed and a more current architecture. While it's true that a higher clock speed can theoretically result in higher frame rates, other factors such as cooling, memory speed, and the number of cores are also as important.

Stream Processors, CUDA Cores, and Compute Units. These terms refer to the core counts found in different graphics card architectures. CUDA Cores are used by Nvidia, while Stream Processors and Compute Units are terms used by AMD. These numbers, like clock speed, aren't really helpful on their own. At best, they help you determine the differences in speed and performance between the same architecture.

Bandwidth or Memory Speed. Just like the two previous specs, this isn't as indicative of performance on its own. However, just like cores and clock speed, a higher bandwidth can contribute to better GPU performance than the other. A DDR6 GPU is significantly faster than a DDR5 one, all others equal.

The Matter of Ray Tracing

Aside from these specs, there are other features that you might want to check depending on how you plan to use your GPU, game-wise. Not all cards, for example, will support VR, so if you plan to do some virtual reality gaming you should aim for at least a mid-range card or better. There's also AI support, for more modern games.

Then, of course, there's ray tracing — hailed by some to be the greatest graphics-related development in recent years. That is, if only we see it in more games.

Ray tracing is a technology used to portray light in 3D scenes in a more lifelike manner. If you want a demonstration of what ray tracing could do, check out some of the greatest CGI work in TV and the movies — these works use ray tracing in order to make even the most fictional of worlds real.

Ray tracing is so revolutionary — and technologically-demanding — because it traces every single ray of light from every single light source in the scene (hence the name). Light may seem to be a... well *light* matter, but considering that how it moves affects everything else on the screen, it takes massive computing power in order to process.

This is also the reason why so few games use this newfangled technology. Most of the games that use it only do so to render shadows and reflections, instead of full-blown scenes. Once it becomes more mainstream, however, we will start seeing ultra-realistic, lifelike scenes in our games. Remember that light not only affects shadows and reflections, but also colors, translucent, and much more.

Today, realistic-looking 3D games use shaders in order to render scenes. Indeed, you'll find a lot of mention of shaders in gaming parlance, though it's not really something you need to look into deeper. Right now all you need to know is that if you want to play the latest and greatest games at the highest possible quality, you would need to buy a ray tracing-capable GPU.

How about setting up dual GPUs?

Graphics cards tend to stick out like a sore thumb in most common PC builds, simply because they produce the highest levels of heat and noise. This makes a good cooling solution very important (more on this later). This also makes it pretty weird to even want two of these behemoths in the same case! "The more, the merrier" isn't true for everything in your PC.

While it's true that there are a few advantages to a dual-GPU setup, this is usually more trouble than it's worth. Gone was the fad of multi-card setup support for games, so right now the best course of action is to get the single best card you can buy. Second cards aren't really significant upgrades.

Speaking of upgrades, don't rely on overclocking graphic cards in order to squeeze more frames into your game. Most graphic cards only allow for up to a 10% improvement boost when overclocked, so when you really want to take things to the next level, you need a better graphics card.

Gaming The Picture

Finally, we arrive at the satisfying level of fine-tuning that comes with tinkering with in-game graphics options.

Note that the options you will see here do not appear only in the games themselves, but also in the GPU-related software that gets installed on your PC. Both Nvidia and AMD have their own specialized apps that allow for the fine-tuning of various graphic settings, most of which will be discussed here.

Note that the terms discussed here are the most common settings, discussed in terms that are as non-technical as possible — there are some very fine-tuned settings available for tinkering if you wish. There's nothing better than experimenting yourself to see just how these settings affect your gaming experience, but just so you don't make any fatal changes to your system it's great to know at least the basics. You know, just like that time you scanned only the first page of an appliance's manual before using it.

Frames per Second (FPS). (Not to be confused with the other "FPS" that appears in this book, which stands for First Person Shooter.) This is arguably the most important setting since it directly affects your gaming experience. It's also directly related to your monitor's refresh rate, as explained earlier.

Remember the movies? Not Netflix (or wherever you get your movies these days). I mean the cinema, where a film consisting of a very long series of still images is projected onto the silver screen, to give the illusion of movement. Each of the still images is a "frame", and the more frames are projected on the screen per second the smoother the action is.

The same holds true for monitors. Each "frame" is a still picture that is projected onto the screen and into our eyes. These frames, when chained together, allow us to perceive movement. Typically, videos are displayed at a minimum of 24 frames per second in order to be smooth. Anything less than that and the eye can perceive a certain "choppiness" that cuts into the experience.

But video games are not typical videos. They often have lots of things going on on the screen at once, and that's why they require higher fps ratings than regular videos.

This setting is related to refresh rate, since the latter acts as the upper-limits at which fps can be displayed. Let's take a gaming-standard 60Hz monitor, for example. This monitor updates at a maximum rate of 60 times per second. That means it can also display a maximum of 60 frames per second and no more. If you are running a game that has 120fps, and your monitor is only a 60Hz one, that means it cannot display all the 120 frames that your PC is outputting. Effectively, you're only viewing 60 frames per second, since the monitor does not refresh fast enough to display the remaining frames. In the same way, it is possible to have a

120Hz monitor and a 60fps game running, without any unusual visual artifacts. Your monitor will continue refreshing as it should even if the game isn't feeding it any new frames.

Of course, it goes without saying that the more fps you squeeze out of your game, the bigger the burden to your graphics card will be. This means that it will have more difficulty rendering bigger pictures, and vice versa. This is why gamers are sometimes split into the high-fps type for maximum response times or the high-res type for bigger and prettier screens. The former sacrifices some image quality, while the latter sacrifices some responsiveness. There is, of course, the middle-ground — you can play a pretty full-HD (1080p) game at 60fps for starters. If you're aiming for the extreme, it's possible to go 4K on 120fps, but anything higher will have trade-offs in visual quality.

Not all games will give you a way to determine your fps, so third-party software may be needed. FRAPS or Riva Tuner can be used with most older games. Steam also lets you view the fps for all your games launched through the platform. But if a way to check fps is available in-game, that's your best bet.

Remember, however, that higher fps won't necessarily give you the best time when gaming. That's strictly between you and your game, with the hardware being a mere bridge. In real-life, a vast majority of gamers are content with 60fps, without any performance penalty. In fact, until recent years, 30fps was the standard for console gaming! Unless you're battling to the death with other gamers, a higher fps isn't needed for enjoyment. The higher fps settings are often reserved for aficionados and competitors. Between these groups, it's only the latter that really needs it, since a missed frame can be the difference between victory and defeat. Realistically speaking, putting a 144fps game in the hands of the everyday gamer is like giving a first-time driver a Maserati. It's nice to have, but it's expensive and impractical.

V-Sync. Have you experienced moving your in-game camera horizontally, only to have the upper half of your screen display a non-matching image to the lower half? This break in the picture is called "screen-tearing", which is something often seen when V-Sync is not turned on.

In a nutshell, V-Sync is a technology used to lock the game's fps to the screen's refresh rate. When these two are in syn, screen tearing disappears and images are always in alignment. Since frames are "scanned" vertically, tearing appears horizontally when the change of frames and the monitor's refresh aren't in step.

While turning on V-Sync eliminates the issue of screen-tearing, it is also at the root of some in-game issues. Essentially, V-Sync tells the game to stop feeding info to the screen before the latter's refresh. This prevents any change of frames in-between refresh, causing the tear. However, because it tells the game to stop sending data, it also results in decreased responsiveness in-game — not something you would want when you need to be agile. Sometimes, turning on V-Sync results in a noticeable lag even when just moving your mouse.

Another issue with V-Sync is the fact that when gaming, fps is never really constant. When there are many things happening on the screen, the frame rate may slow down as the CPU+GPU has a harder time trying to crunch and churn out data. The way V-Sync works, not only limits the game's frame rate to match the monitor's — it also limits it to a set

143

value if it falls below the monitor's refresh rate. For example, if you have a 60Hz monitor displaying a 60fps game (V-Sync limited) and the game slows down, V-Sync will lock the game to a set value (like, say, 30fps). Once the game speeds up, V-Sync amps it up to 60fps again. When this happens frequently enough, it results in a visual stutter that rains on your gaming experience.

With all these downsides, many gamers prefer to leave V-Sync off. But it's undeniable that V-Sync has something going for it. So to resolve V-Sync's weaknesses, various technologies have been developed...

Adaptive V-Sync. This is a technology created by Nvidia, which resolves the stutter caused by the frame rate jumping from a very high to a very low number. When activated, it disables V-Sync when it goes below the monitor's refresh rate. You can access this through the Nvidia control panel. This allows you to keep V-Sync on without any weird stutters.

FreeSync and G-Sync. This is a couple of rival V-Sync replacements made by AMD and Nvidia, respectively. This takes on a different idea and requires a compatible graphics card and monitor to work.

Basically, it allows the monitor's refresh rate to adjust with the frame rate of the game you're playing, instead of the other way around. Of course, there's a limit to how high the monitor's refresh rate can go, but adapting the monitor to the fps eliminates all of the problems that the original V-Sync presents.

In a bid for total graphics card domination, Nvidia has made some of its GeForce cards work with select FreeSync monitors. However, AMD has not yet done the same for G-Sync, so Nvidia takes a leap forward when it comes to compatibility.

Anti-Aliasing. This is an umbrella term that refers to the technology used to smooth out the jagged edges of what are supposed to be curved objects on-screen. This technology has been around for some time, and various solutions exist for anti-aliasing.

You will see "aliasing" when you look at curved objects and see tiny little staircases on them, instead of smooth lines. Anti-aliasing works by blending the colors of these pixels, with the surroundings to make them disappear, making things appear smooth. This little eye-candy can be somewhat demanding on your graphics card, so if you're playing an already graphics-heavy game, turning on anti-aliasing can result in performance drops.

There may be different types of anti-aliasing available to you, and each of them has different performance levels. One of the most taxing is SSAA, or Supersampling Anti-Aliasing (just the name is taxing!). If you must eliminate the staircases but your graphics card is already screaming in pain, choose any of the other ones instead (TXAA, MLAA, MFAA, MSAA, SMAA, or FXAA — though the last one tends to blur out edges instead of smooth them out). What options you have will depend on the type of GPU you have. If you have the latest generation of Nvidia cards and you really want to push the limits, you can turn on DLSS (Deep Learning Super-Sampling — the name says it all) and experience the next generation of anti-aliasing.

Anti-aliasing also lends itself to various adjustments, often in multiples of 2 (2x, 4x, etc.). This refers to the number of color samples the system is taking — the higher the number, the more samples and therefore the more accurate the anti-aliasing. This, of course, leads to greater strain on your graphics card.

Often, gamers have two places wherein they can turn on anti-aliasing — the game itself, and the graphics card control panel. Generally, turning the AA options on in the latter will override the former, but that is not often the case. That's why a little experimentation is sometimes in order.

Of course, since higher resolutions mean smaller pixels, getting a good monitor allows you to have a smooth experience even without turning anti-aliasing on. Just don't get too close or you'll still notice them.

Rendering Resolution. When you see this option, that means you can either upscale or downsample the image on-screen to fit your monitor's native resolution. For example, let's say you have a 4k monitor. However, the game is only being rendered at 1440p. Turning on upscaling means your game will be blown up to fit your monitor. It's not always fun, though, as the UI also gets blown up and the game pretty much gets in your face. That's another reason to match your monitor's specs with that of the PC itself.

On the other hand, it's possible to render the game at 1440p and have a monitor that's only 1080p. When downsampling is activated, the game is compressed to HD, and everything will look better than when just rendering the game at 1080p. However, the graphics card takes quite a hit when this is done, so don't use it unless you have the juice to spare.

Field of View (FOV). This is a strictly in-game setting since its existence would depend on the type of game you are playing. Similar to the FOV concept on cameras, the field of view defines the angle at which the elements of the game can be seen. Imagine your monitor as your virtual lens into the world of the game (because it is) — the bigger the FOV, the more you can see from each side. The field of view is measured in degrees, and a bigger number means a wider angle.

While this is something you would want to have in an FPS game so you can have more situational awareness, it has two caveats. First, it can be demanding on your GPU, and second, a bigger FOV pushes the center of the screen farther away. The latter means you have to be more precise in your mouse actions to make sure you're hitting the target.

Depth of Field (DOF). This is another set inspired by photography. You know how those photographs blur those in the background so the subject in the foreground is focused? That's achieved by adjusting the depth of field. A smaller DOF means a blurred background, while a high DOF value means everything is sharp as the foreground.

Intuitively, a high DOF setting will consume more processing power than a regular DOF setting. Having that movie-like blur in the background might seem more natural, but again depending on the game you can adjust this so you can see much farther into the horizon.

High Dynamic Range (HDR). Yet other graphics tweak that came directly from the world of photography, HDR determines how bright "bright" can be, and how dark "dark" is. Turning the feature off (or having a low value) can result in dark shadows that don't reveal enough detail. This can also happen in brightly-lit locations in the game, where the light seems to swallow up everything.

Aside from your graphics card, your monitor is another important factor that determines whether you can — or should — go for HDR. Monitors incapable of good contrast values cannot really display the contrasting light and shadow that will appear once HDR is cranked up.

Motion Blur. Have you noticed the blur left behind when someone moves as you click your camera's shutter button? That's what motion blur is. Most gamers turn this off since it's not particularly good-looking. It also causes some frame drops when turned on. There are racing game fans who like to keep this turned on, however, to add a touch of realism.

Filtering. This set comes in different varieties. Essentially, texture filtering defines how your game's textures are displayed on the 3D assets. Think of textures as 2D wrapping paper positioned around a 3D box. Because the 2D asset is superimposed over the 3D, the computer cannot immediately know the values for a specific pixel in the texture as it can be viewed at different angles or distances. It's similar to how the designs (pattern, shapes, colors, shine, etc.) of a gift box may appear different depending on which angle you view it from, despite the whole texture being made from a single spread of paper.

One of the most basic forms of filtering is the bilinear method, which samples the four nearest pixels to the pixel in question to get the latter's value. An improvement upon this, called trilinear filtering, does the same but also samples textures of different types to make sure they blend in properly. Trilinear filtering is used on "mipmaps" — lower-resolution textures used in displaying distant objects on-screen. Just like in real-life, distant objects appear more blurry than closer ones. Mipmaps are used to reflect this phenomenon, and trilinear filtering ensures there is no jarring break between the high-res textures of nearby items and the low-res ones of distant objects.

But that's not yet the end of our texturing woes. Objects that are seen from oblique angles should be filtered differently in order to improve clarity, since using the previous two methods would only work if we are looking at objects straight on. Once we move on to the side, the texture quickly becomes blurry, since the way we're looking at the object is not supported by either bilinear or trilinear filtering. This is where anisotropic filtering steps in, allowing us to see textures consistently no matter what angle we see them from.

Because anisotropic filtering is essential to the enjoyment of almost all modern games, most don't even include an option to turn it off. But if your PC is screaming in pain while running the game and there *is* an option to turn it off or lessen its values, it's worthwhile to consider it. Like anti-aliasing, anisotropic filtering comes in values in multiples of two. Either 8x or 16x is the sweet spot for those with capable systems. It's not a very GPU-intensive task, but if you need to make the game run more smoothly you can sacrifice the graphics at 1x (no filtering). A blasphemy for graphics purists, but hey, whatever works! We're the PC Master Race for a reason.

Ambient Occlusion. If you noticed by now that the most important graphics settings depend on how in-game rays of light are interpreted by your machine, you are absolutely right. And ambient occlusion is no different.

In the real world, even in an evenly-lit room, there are areas that appear darker than others because they are reached by less light. Ambient occlusion tries to emulate this in in-game scenes by adding a layer of soft shadows in places that are out of reach by the room's primary light source. This results in a more realistic render of whatever's on-screen. It's a more GPU-friendly alternative to the more realistic (but more taxing) real-time shadow rendering.

Like with anti-aliasing, there are also different kinds of ambient occlusion. The first is SSAO, introduced in one of the most graphically-taxing games ever made — *Crysis*. Surprisingly, it doesn't hit your game's performance that much, so if you have a mid-range PC you may want to leave it on for more realism. It's pretty much the standard for major games nowadays. The other, HBAO (also evolved into HDAO and HBAO+) is much more taxing since there are more areas taken into account when computing for areas that will be darkened. It's more accurate, but don't switch to this unless you have a sufficiently-powerful system.

Bloom. This is the phenomenon in which light seeps in from a source, much like how bright sunlight drowns the edges of a window in real-life. It would have been good, had not some games abused the option and added it despite poor implementation. You might see walls that suddenly look reflective around a light source or candlelights that look like house fires. If this is the case, there's no harm in turning the feature off.

Tessellation. This is a complex process that adds extra depth and complexity to the in-game objects. The results might not immediately be apparent when looking at smooth surfaces, but textures will appear more pronounced and realistic when tessellation is turned on.

As with bloom, however, how well tessellation helps the game will depend on how well it was made by its developers. In some cases, it doesn't even make a noticeable improvement. For this, just test out the setting in your game to determine whether or not you'd like to leave it turned on.

Quality Settings. This is by far the most common type of graphic setting for games. Unlike the previous settings, however, what it does will vary depending on the game. Essentially, quality settings come as a bundle that can change anything from textures to shadows.

Quality settings can be toggled from Low to High, with each step upwards improving the game's assets. Because many things are being changed at once, even a single step up can have a noticeable effect on performance. Determining what's best for your system will depend on its specs and the demands of the game, so do a little experimenting. If you have a lower-end machine, though, it might be best to leave quality settings too Low to at least have decent responsiveness.

Remember that everything in this chapter so far is just recommendatory — the actual graphics settings you should select will solely depend on what you have. Because of a wide variety of factors, the same game may perform differently even on the same PCs. It all depends on the individual parts, and how they are optimized. By parts, of course, I mean both the hardware and software.

Speaking of hardware... isn't it about time we address the elephant in the room? You've learned how to optimize Windows, where to get all sorts of games, and even how to set up game graphics for the best possible performance. But what about the rest of the computer? How do you tune it up? How do you get on for cheap if you're upgrading? Better yet. How do you *build* one from scratch if you want to truly embrace the world of PCs?

All this and more right when you turn the page!

CHAPTER 6: Getting Your Hands Dirty: The Many Ways to Get A PC

It's true what may have been lurking at the back of your mind since you started this book — the world of gaming, especially on PC, can sometimes be elitist. As in any niche, there will always be bad eggs who look down on others whose "gear" they deem is inferior. "Oh you're a PC gamer? What do you have for graphics? Intel... UHD 600?! Okay... excuse me while I barf."

But this isn't how it's meant to be. The very reason why gaming evolved on PC was so that it can be accessible to anyone and everyone. So what if you can't build a PC (though at the end of this chapter you would already know how)? There are always shops and even whole companies who could do it for you. The second part of this chapter will be dedicated to this. But first, let's have a rundown of the different parts of a PC:

CPU. This is the Central Processing Unit, and as the name says is the most important part of the PC. The CPU is the brain of the machine, the part that does all the billions of computations that the computer has to do.

As you most likely already know, the most important spec you need to look for in a CPU will be the number of cores. These determine how many processes your PC can do at the same time — the more the merrier! The overall CPU speed will also depend on the architecture, with more modern models being faster (and less power-hungry) than older ones. Of course, there are also clock speeds which is the speed at which each of the cores can perform its tasks.

Because CPUs can now be easily overclocked (with their own limitations), clock speeds are no longer as much a limitation as they were before.

There are only two major CPU brands that you need to be aware of — Intel and (once more) AMD. Intel *used to be* the leader in the processor game, historically producing some of history's most powerful and efficient processors (albeit at a higher cost). Intel processors are famous for their long-term reliability, and the brand itself used to mean the most premium CPUs on the market. In recent years, however, Intel has also made its mark on the budget PC segment, allowing anyone accesses to the vaunted quality that is Intel. If you're gaming, though, aim for at the very least an Intel i3 as your starting gear. If you're planning to upgrade, you can go as high as the brand's top-of-the-line i9, which is plenty powerful enough to catch anything you can throw at it.

For a long time, AMD's name had only played second-fiddle to Intel. They were known for producing low-cost CPUs, but you only get as much as you pay for. With the advent of the Ryzen series, however, AMD has barged into the processor arena with a challenge Intel can't ignore. Ryzen's names are even made to equal that of Intel — Ryzen 3 being the entry-level, and capable of light gaming. AMD distinguishes the upper echelons of its processor line with the provocative name "Threadripper", recommended if you want an alternative for the i9.

RAM. Second to the CPU in terms of importance, a good Random Access Memory module speeds up your PC by storing ongoing processes and follow-ups. Games are notoriously reliant on good RAM, because of the many millions of processes needed to display what you see on-screen. For graphics-intensive games, at least 8GB RAM is recommended. The most basic games can run on a 2GB system, but you tend to sacrifice a lot of responsiveness.

Thankfully, no company has a monopoly (or duopoly) on RAM modules. Whichever brand you choose, however, you need to be aware of two important specs: type and speed. Thanks to limitations of the CPU and motherboard (that large circuit where everything is attached), PCs can only have certain RAM types and speeds. Upgrading to an unsupported RAM module could mean wasting money (the same goes for CPUs, but CPUs aren't upgraded as often as RAM modules).

RAM modules have different data-rate standards, and this is called its "Type". The current standard is DDR4 RAM, which is faster and more capable than its predecessor DDR3. Just like CPUs, the RAM's speed is measured in MHz. This measures how quickly information and instructions can be shuffled in and out of the memory. Going for DDR4 is a safe bet especially when gaming, since the more powerful the RAM the better it can handle heavy applications. If you're working under a budget constraint, however, you can still find games that run under DDR3.

Storage. This one needs no introduction, but it's still important to plan out your plan for your PC's memory. Storage is one of the most versatile options since it can come in multiple forms.

The most common (and older) form is the standard HDD, or Hard Disk Drive. This is your parents' storage of choice — that thin spinning metal disk housed in a bulky casing. It's still ideal for the storage of large file collections, such as movies, images, and games that you rarely use. While generally slower than the current crop of SSDs, the HDD is very cost-efficient and does not suffer from the same lifespan problem as SSDs.

SSDs or Solid State Drives should be your go-to for frequently-accessed items, and the Windows system itself. Unlike HDDs that have a spinning disk inside, solid-state devices are technically overpowered flash drives that operate purely through circuits (hence the name "solid-state"). SSDs are much faster, though they tend to be more expensive than their HDD counterparts. Even if you can afford large-capacity SSDs, it's still advisable to reserve them only for files that you need to access often due to the technology's limited lifespan. By "limited" we mean that it lasts for a few years before you start experiencing any problems — still it's better to be prudent and future-proof your PC.

The ideal storage device should at least be 120GB for your main, which should be enough to house a few memory-intensive games. If you're only playing on emulators, even this would be plenty enough (unless you also have a large and frequently-accessed media collection). For a secondary drive (HDD) you can push it a little further and get a 500GB drive at least.

Ports. I don't think many beginner PC buyers pay attention to the importance of ports, and that's because you can usually buy an extension, hub, or adapter to cover anything you're missing. Still, it's best to make sure you have everything you need to avoid the expense and hassle of buying something extra.

The most common port is, of course, the ubiquitous USB. It is the port used by a majority of modern peripherals, from the keyboard and mouse to printers. Of course, you'll also be aiming to use the USB port for your controllers, so make sure you have some extra. But not all USBs are equal, though, so pay attention to which generation you're getting. USB 4 is the current generation, and it's very different from the previous USB generations in that it's faster and much slimmer. Whereas we're used to seeing the rectangular ports until USB 3.1, USB 4 looks like the USB-C ports we see on mobile phones. This large difference can cause a lot of compatibility issues, so it's best to stick with the more common blue ports. The bleeding edge isn't always easy to be on. Besides, the old Type A rectangular ports are backward compatible with earlier versions, so you enjoy a wider array of functions from all your drivers and peripherals.

Another important port will be audio. Depending on whether you will be using voice chat when gaming (like in Discord), you might want to take advantage of separate audio in and out jacks. Some PCs have special features built into these ports to improve incoming and outgoing sound quality.

Of course, you also need a video port that is compatible with the display you will be using. Older devices still make use of VGA ports, which still works if you're not after anything graphics-intensive. Still, either DisplayPort or HDMI would be the best as they provide the best quality and are very widely supported. Note, though that the video port would only be a separate concern if you don't have a discrete graphics card loaded in since these cards carry their own ports.

Networking ports are also important, as most computers are just dead weight without the Internet. Go for wired as much as possible, for a stable signal — for this you'll need an ethernet or RJ45 port. You might also want to check out what kind of WiFi card your PC supports so you can be certain of connectivity. If there isn't any integrated WiFi support, you can always load a separate card onto the PC's PCI-E slot.

Peripherals. Finally, we come to the goodies you attach to your PC. If you think choosing internals takes up a lot of time, just check out how much time you'll spend browsing for the ideal keyboard, mouse, monitor, earphone, webcam, and the like.

In the end, simply choose what's right for you, but be wary about sinking too much money into a specific peripheral without researching thoroughly. New technologies can make whatever you have now pretty outdated in two years, so always leave room for potential updates.

Buying A Pre-Built PC

Anyone who says building a PC from scratch isn't intimidating would by lying. That's why for the majority of PC gamers who don't want to dive into wires and cards just yet, pre-built PCs exist.

In simplest terms, a pre-built PC is one that someone else has built for you. These can either be made as a part of a production line (like the majority of PCs on the market) or made-to-order devices. First, we'll look at the former, and I'll guide you towards what to look for when buying a pre-built gaming-oriented PC.

What to look for

You already know about PC internals, and all you need to do is find that sweet spot where the PC's performance meets your budget. The good thing with pre-built PCs is that they are often balanced, so there's no performance bottleneck (that phenomenon where one part is hampered by another due to differing performance capacities). But there are a few other factors you should look for. Of course, you'd want the aesthetics to match your taste, and there's an infinite variety of cases to help you with that. You'd also want the design to allow for upgradeability — larger cases mean there's more room for additions or updates. Check as well that there's adequate cooling built-in, as you won't want to start cooking omelets on your PC.

In the next section, I will be listing some of the best pre-built gaming PCs with a simple review. Note that prices are always subject to change without notice. These PC recommendations will cover different price ranges, from the sub-$1,000 range to the I-don't-earn-enough-for-this range. I will also cover various form factors because gaming isn't just confined to the den.

Best Pre-Built Gaming PCs: Laptops

Acer Predator Helios 300. This sub-$1,500 (for the 2019 version) beast has a 9th Generation i7 processor, making it a powerful gaming laptop no matter what genre you're into. The 144Hz screen is just the first in its array of great peripheral hardware, which extends to its durable case and a great selection of ports. You might want to keep the power cord and external HD handy, though, since battery life and storage aren't among its strong suits. There's also a 2020 version, with greatly-improved battery life, though it's a couple of hundred dollars more expensive.

Acer Nitro 5. This 2019 device is just under $800, and sports a 1080p monitor at 60Hz with a Core i5 processor — plenty powerful enough for anything except the most demanding of games. There's also room for expansion, which isn't something you see every day on a laptop.

Acer Nitro 7. Hovering just above the $1,000 mark, the Nitro 7 is the Nitro 5's big brother in almost every way. While its built-in graphics (Nvidia GTX 1650) is overshadowed by competing products from other companies, it does have a sweet 144Hz screen and great battery life. It also offers two expansion slots for storage drives, making it an ideal multimedia center.

MSI GL65. This model comes in different variants (as if the model name isn't confusing enough), and most hover around the neighborhood of $1,400. For this, you get a solid mid-tier Nvidia graphics card, a 1080p screen, great chassis, and overall a great selection of internals. The Leopard 10SFK version has an i7 processor, while the Leopard 10SDK has an i5 — but there are other variants to choose from.

MSI Bravo 15. Also priced at around $1,000, the Bravo 15 has an all-AMD hardware selection, giving it more value than many competitors. It has a 120Hz display with a Ryzen 4000 series processor, and 16GB of RAM or more. There's also support for FreeSync, which cuts away those jittery frame performances. You might want to buy a separate cooling pad for this, though, as it easily gets hot while gaming.

Lenovo Legion Y545. This sub $1,300 laptop has a reasonably good build, on par with Acer's Helios 300. However, it gets hotter than the competition (like, literally), so like the Bravo 15 you might want to buy a cooling pad for this.

Alienware m15 R3. If you're not familiar with the brand, "Alienware" means we're entering the "expensive" category of laptops. This model goes way above $1,500, but it's worth it if you have the money. As far as high-end laptops go, this is still affordable gaming. The aesthetics are great, and the internals is powerful enough to support a 300Hz display. You get the latest generation of i7 CPUs, at least 16GB RAM, and 1TB of storage. All that power does a number on its battery life, though, so keep that charger handy.

Razer Blade 15 Advanced Model. If you want something that's around the same price range as the Alienware but with more juice to last you while unplugged, check out this laptop instead. Its 144Hz display is powered by an RTX 2070 Max-Q graphics card, and it has an i7 under the hood for great gaming performance. You can't have everything, though, and this model also has some issues with heating.

ASUS ROG Zephyrus G14. ASUS's entry into the affordable-yet-premium category has us looking at a 14-inch ultra-portable gaming device. Less expensive than the Alienware, you can take the ASUS pretty much anywhere to enjoy its 120Hz screen powered by an Nvidia GeForce RTX 2060 card. There's also a Ryzen 9 and 16GB of RAM under the hood, so you can game wherever. If you want to push things even further, there's the **Zephyrus S GX502** model that's just as portable but packs a 240Hz screen and substantially more power.

HP Omen X 2S. Aside from being one heck of a laptop, the Omen X 2S is also an excellent conversation starter. This laptop sports a second screen that allows you to have an always-open in-game chatbox. The touchpad placement is unusual but intuitive, and the i7 driven internals provide more than enough power for gaming. It's VR-ready and equipped with an RTX 2070 GPU. Its price is also closer to $2,000, so it's quite an investment.

Acer PredatorTriton 500. This time we have Acer's entry into the >$1,500 range. The 2019 model is more affordable at under $1,500, but the more expensive 2020 one is a better deal thanks to its great hardware. It's got a G-Sync capable 300Hz display and an i7 CPU. You pay for the visuals with short battery life, though, but if you won't be untethered for long then this laptop is a good option.

ASUS ROG Mothership. Just for fun, let's take this section to another level. Or more like another dimension, in terms of price. This freak of technology is a few dollars shy of $9,000, and offers some of the most powerful portable specs anywhere — a 17-inch 144Hz screen, Intel i9 processor, an RTX 2080 GPU, and 128GB of RAM. It's extreme to the core, but it's also unmatched in terms of performance. Even the form factor is different, with a tablet-like touchscreen surface that covers a keyboard. If you're looking for the perfect laptop, then this is the closest you can get. Until, of course, ASUS unveils a follow up.

Best Pre-Built Gaming PCs: Desktops

Acer Aspire TC-885-UA92. After the bill-shock of the Mothership, let's start off with something a little more modest. This sub-$700 desktop does not have its own graphics card, but it does have an i5 and 12GB of RAM. That's plenty of power to play basic games at an appreciable speed and quality. More of an all-around machine than a strictly-gaming PC, it does the job nevertheless.

iBUYPOWER Trace 4 9310. If you want something with the price tag of the Aspire and the capability of a GPU-driven PC, there's this little baby from iBUYPOWER. Powered by AMD all the way (Ryzen 5, Radeon RX 5500 XT) plus 8GB of RAM, this pre-built PC offers a decent compromise between price and quality. If you want something more powerful, you can check out the Element 9260 from the same brand, which offers an i7 and a GTX 1660 with 16GB of RAM.

Skytech Chronos. Speaking of AMD-powered devices, another great device is Skytech's entry-level competitor. Powered by an AMD Ryzen 7 3700X and an RTX 2070 Super GPU, this sub-$1,600 device has 16GB of RAM for gaming agility. If you're into the fancy RGB LEDs that seem to define today's generation of gaming PC cases, you'll also enjoy Skytech's sleek yet colorful aesthetics. If you like the looks and have the budget, Skytech also has a more extreme gaming model with Ryzen 9, RTX 3090 GPU, and 64GB RAM — the **Prism II**, at above $4,000.

Dell G5. This one's pretty much the Intel equivalent of the Chronos. The Dell G4 also has a price tag of just under $1,600, but with that, you're getting an i7 processor and a GeForce RTX 2060 graphics card. There's also 16GB of RAM on board, so you get excellent gaming performance.

MSI MEG Trident X. Stepping up from the previous entries (except the Prism II) both in terms of price and performance, the MEG Trident X is among the best gaming PCs for the money. At a little under $2,800, you get an i7 beast with an RTX 3080 GPU and 32GB of RAM. Not too much of an overkill in terms of specs, but perfectly comfortable even in the face of demanding games. What's even better is that the Trident X comes in a compact form factor, so your rig taking up too much space is not an issue.

Zotac Mek Mini. Speaking of space-saving, there's an even smaller PC out there that does not compromise in terms of raw gaming power. Priced at under $1,800, the Zotac Mek Mini is filled to the brim with an i7 processor and an RTX

2070 GPU. It also has 16GB of RAM, placing it squarely in the mid-range category. While the small space means you're not able to customize the internals as much as its larger competitors, the size gives it a fair advantage for those needing to squeeze their gaming apparatus in tighter space.

Corsair Vengeance a4100. Priced just a hair shy of $2,000, this is a pretty expensive machine loaded with a Ryzen 7 3700X, an RTX 2070 GPU, and 16GB of RAM. But if you're a streamer (or planning to), this might be your best bet thanks to its built-in Elgato 4K60 PRO capture card. Capture cards are an important part of a streamer's gear, taking the brunt of the processes needed to capture footage while still maintaining a smooth gaming experience. With this model, you can game at the highest quality settings *and* capture the same for broadcast to all your wowed fans.

Alienware Aurora R11. Of course, we just had to squeeze an Alienware build into this list, if only to top it off. Thankfully this one isn't *that* expensive (a little under $2,800), especially after the Skytech Prism II. Still, it managed to pack a Core i9 processor and an RTX 3090 GPU, plus 64GB of RAM for a smooth experience no matter which game you decide to load. It's also pretty customizable, but don't use it around anyone who hates the hum of CPU cooling fans. This model's coolers tend to get loud.

Remember that in this section, I recommended mostly PCs that are *especially* geared towards gaming. But note that, as I said in the first chapter, virtually *any* PC can be used to game. You just need to adjust the settings and tweak them appropriately so that the game can be run smoothly. Heck, it's even possible to emulate the whole PS1 library (as well as those of older consoles) using one of those ultra-cheap micro-PCs that attach to the back of your living room TV.

Case in point: the baseball-sized **Chuwi LarkBox** that retails for under $200 and loaded with nothing more than an Intel J4125 and 6GB RAM. You can even play minor games here, too, if you don't mind the longer-than-usual reload times. So if all of the options above are out of your reach, and you still want to try your hands at gaming, don't fret — just get *literally* any PC and you can enjoy PC gaming in at least some of its many flavors.

Best Pre-Built Gaming PCs: Custom-Built PCs

What if you have a specific set of specs in mind, but you can't find the right PC for it? What can you do? You ask someone to build that PC for you, that's what. Provided you have a clear vision of what gaming rig you'd like to have, plus a little extra in your savings to pay for overhead costs, you can design and build your PC from the comfort of your own home, without getting your hands the least bit dirty.

This endeavor, unlike simply adding a pre-built PC to your online shopping cart, requires at least some knowledge of *how* PCs are built by hand. This is because custom-built PC makers let you choose your own parts for the final product, and though their online tools have safeguards in place to make sure you don't mix and match incompatible ones, it's still better to know how to do this properly. We're going to leave the exact how-tos until the next section (which details how to build your own PC from scratch). For now, we'll just focus on some of the best companies and services that offer custom PC builds.

Xidax. Perhaps the least-famous company on this list, this is nevertheless one of the best places to start if you're looking for custom builds. First of all, they provide some of the most affordable PCs in the class, with builds starting out under $600. Don't even ask about how high the other end of this price range can go — the sky's pretty much the limit with these custom-built devices. They offer devices for various use cases too, with workstations and professional PCs in addition to gaming. For those who want a more portable option, Xidax also offers custom-built laptops through the flexibility in choosing parts is understandably less than that of desktops.

Xidax offers customization not just for basic components but also for aesthetics and performance improvement. You can request your CPUs and GPUs to be overclocked, and RGB lights installed in the PC's case. You can even request engraving for a truly customized look!

Xidax also offers other great buying options, such as extended warranty periods and monthly installments through Affirm.

CyberPowerPC. This is also a good place to start with, as the company offers gaming-oriented rigs starting at under $800. They also have an Amazon storefront for their pre-built devices, which start for much less. Another good thing about this company is that they offer a really wide range of base models, so you could choose one which is more fine-tuned to your preferences.

CyberPowerPC has good after sales support, offering lifetime tech support and a 3-year service plan. Their build and shipping time leaves a few things to be desired, but if you're ordering on Amazon you can have priority though Amazon Prime. They also offer monthly installments through Affirm.

Digital Storm. This is another company that offers pre-built devices on the cheap. Their base models will set you back around $700, and that's already suitable for minor gaming. Of course there are plenty of things that can be upgraded, even though the base range of models are fewer than that of CyberPowerPC or our next entry, iBuyPower.

Digital Storm stands out in the warranty game, allowing you to upgrade your warranty to a maximum of 5 years. The company also offers financing options, so you can make installment payments as well.

iBuyPower. A familiar name from our earlier list of pre-built desktops, iBuyPower is the closest competitor to the two options above. iBuyPower offers pretty much the same level of services, from the price range to the product range. They even have a similar Amazon storefront!

Perhaps the only distinction is the wider range of customization options offered by iBuyPower in terms of aesthetics. They also offer an upsell for warranty, in case you'd want to have an additional layer of protection for your investment. They also have a rush option for the build and shipment, so you can get your device faster.

MainGear. MainGear's offerings seem a little lackluster in the field of custom-built PCs, but they deserve a look nonetheless. They offer all the works that their competitors do, and their prices are not bad either. The starting model is just a little over $800.

Aside from offering warranty upgrades, the company also has a Prime-eligible Amazon storefront that lets you get your PC much faster than other services.

Origin PC. If you want to focus exclusively on the other end of the price spectrum, look no further than Origin PC. The company offers only mid- to high-end PCs, with their cheapest models just below the $1,500 mark. The company was created by former Alienware employees, so that alone should give you a hint about their specialization. What sets them apart is the fine-grained control they offer over almost everything from the color of the chassis to the form factor of your PC. They also have a more premium lineup of peripherals than many competitors on this list.

Origin offers excellent customization options, along with advanced options for shipping and warranty. You can also check their Amazon storefront for pre-built options. The company also offers free tech support for life, along with installment payments.

Falcon Northwest. Speaking of PC builders with a history, none has a past more respectable than Falcon Northwest. The company debuted in 1992, making it among the oldest custom builders on the Internet. These guys also created the whole concept of the "gaming PC" back when PCs were either just business machines or everyday workhorses. The whole PC Master Race should tip their hats in respect!

They also pride themselves on something that few other builders could boast of — they assemble every PC by hand, using the absolute most premium materials and the most rigorous testing methods. By that alone, you know that their quality won't come cheap.

Indeed, Falcon's cheapest PCs start at above $2,000, with a lot of room for upgrades. They also offer a lot of customization options, along with a hefty 3-year warranty on their devices. And just to drive home the fact that they aren't any budget company, they don't even offer monthly installments or any other financing options. But if you want some of the best custom-made pre-built PCs money can buy — the type of PC that even government agencies rave about — then Falcon Northwest is the best place to go.

BLD. Another custom-built PC company with a pedigree (backed by PC hardware company NZXT), BLD offers some high-quality PCs with a twist — instead of asking you to select from customizable base models, BLD's site will take you through a series of questions that will assess the type of PC that is best suited to your needs. It even asks what main game you wish to play and how much you're willing to spend, and cooks up a recommendation from your answers!

The recommended system is still configurable, but the painless way you get to the recommendation is heaven-sent for newbies who find the constant slew of model numbers from various PC parts intimidating. Perhaps the only limitation is that most of the peripherals (especially the cases) show only NZXT options. Not that it's much to complain about since some builders don't even offer options for cases... and Terry Crews himself used an NZXT case for his custom PC build.

They also build fast — all systems are guaranteed to go out within 48 hours, and there's even an option for same-day shipping (for an extra $200). If you want a custom PC and want it now, this is the place for you.

AVADirect. This is the weirdest one on this list because it's more of a PC supermarket than a dedicated custom-builder. While AVADirect offers an array of custom-built PCs and laptops, they also offer various other hardware from peripherals to tablets. That's great if you want a one-stop-shop for all your PC needs.

Like most others, AVADirect offers monthly installments for their system, which might come in handy since their base models are fairly expensive, with the cheapest being just a few bucks shy of $1,000.

Unless you already know exactly what you want — say the premium options of Falcon Northwest or the expediency of NZXT — it's best to check out all of these sites first before making your final choice. Note as well that there are LOTS of other custom-built PC companies out there, and there might even be some in your neighborhood. Even though we're primarily thinking of these PCs as instruments of leisure and play, it's still wise to treat their purchase as investments. Who knows how else your PC can serve you in the future.

Building Your Own PC

Finally, we come to the most technical part of this book. Now, I know some of you think that this chapter isn't even necessary — after all, you could just go to the nearest BestBuy and grab yourself a PC, or have one shipped to you through eBay or Amazon. So what's the big deal?

Well, young grasshopper, there's a simple answer: PC building is an art and a science. Yes, it's challenging — just like your 10th-grade science paper. Yes, it's easy to bungle — just like that first time you tried holding a brush to a canvas. But it's oh-so-worth-it. You not only get unparalleled flexibility and the possibility of savings, but you also get to know more about how computers work *and* get that incredible satisfaction of building something that's true of your own. Just like how a seasoned warrior seeks to create a weapon that's truly his own, spend enough time around a computer and you'd get that itch to craft one yourself.

Of course, however, it takes time, patience, and a certain degree of fearlessness. Now, I can't give any of that to you, but what I can give is the knowledge you need to brave this new quest. And you'll be in good company, too — just type "build PC" in YouTube's search bar and you get hundreds of videos of people chronicling their own PC-building adventures. Even Superman Henry Cavill and Brooklyn Nine-Nine's Terry Crews are in on the trend! And yes, of course, Terry Crews used an Old Spice bottle for his build, because why the heck not!

Finding the parts

The first step to a great PC build is to make sure you get all the right parts. There are lots of things to consider here — you'd not only need parts that are capable enough and suited to your budget, but you also need to ensure compatibility above all things.

We've already covered the basics of the various computer parts early in this chapter, so let's go into a few more details. Remember that for each PC part you'd have an unearthly number of choices across several manufacturers, but as long as you keep to the guidelines below, you'll be fine:

CPU. It's just Intel and AMD here, and it's all down to preference. The current crop of processors has put AMD at a slight lead when it comes to efficiency and cost-effectiveness, but Intel still leads when it comes to features. However, note that whichever camp you choose, you will *not* be able to switch to the other later down the road unless you also change your motherboard. The motherboard is geared to work only with the socket type of a specific CPU series from either AMD or Intel, so you need to make sure they match each other.

Motherboard. As mentioned, certain motherboard models only cater to certain types of CPUs because of their sockets. For example, a top-level AMD TRX40 motherboard can carry all processors that have the sTRX4 socket. That means only AMD, and not Intel. There's also intra-brand compatibility to check — the aforementioned TRX40 is compatible with current future releases of AMD's Threadripper processors, but not with older generations.

Note as well that there are various motherboard form factors, such as ATX, E-ATX, Mini-ITX, and Micro-ATX... all the way down to the minuscule Pico-ITX for small appliances. Smaller form factors mean a smaller footprint, but you will have less space to expand on components. For gaming, a full-sized ATX is recommended.

Case. Many people think that the case is just for aesthetics, but aside from the form factor and the flashy lights, you need to ensure that you have enough space for the things you want to install.

Storage, RAM, and GPU. The faster and the more modern, the better for both — but you need to make sure that they fit inside the motherboard and the case! Storage devices are a particular pain if you have a small case since sometimes you can't use the 3.5-inch bays intended for HDDs if something else (such as the PSU) is blocking it.

PSU. This is the part that converts the power from the outlet to the power that the PC can use. The more powerful the specs of the PC are, the more powerful the PSU needs to be (and the more power it draws, so watch your bill!). Less powerful PCs can get away with 500W or thereabouts, but more powerful PCs can go up to 1000W or more. Since calculating the PC's power requirements isn't easy, you can

Google for "PC Power Supply Calculator" to make things a lot easier. The one from OuterVision is particularly good.

CPU Cooler. Most CPUs have their own thermal paste and cooling fan that you can use out of the box. But if you're aiming for a more powerful build, you might want a specialized cooler to make sure your PC is running smoothly and quietly. You can choose between simple air coolers and AIO (all-in-one, liquid-based) coolers, with the latter being more expensive. Make sure the cooler still fits your case, as some of them may be quite large.

Since selecting the parts of your PC is all about knowing their compatibility with each other, I recommend using an online compatibility checker to ensure that your parts will work together once you have them on hand. PC Part Picker has set the golden standard for these tools, and typing in your components in their checker can save you from a lot of headaches down the road.

And since we're on the subject of online tools, pay a visit to PC Builds' Bottleneck Calculator as well — this tool helps you make a balanced computer system that makes the best use of all its parts. A PC is said to have a bottleneck when one or more of its parts lags behind in terms of performance, therefore reducing the overall performance of the system. The PC may be more than a sum of its parts, but when the parts are bad the whole system goes down.

Getting the Tools

What a joy it would be if all computers can just be snapped together like Lego blocks! But it's not a perfect world, so you need a few things with which to tinker:

Screwdriver. Get both a Philips head (for most components and mounting screws) and a flat head (for coolers, sometimes).

Scissors and Cable ties. These are very important to organize the hectic mass of cables that will come with your PC. Sometimes, a cable solution is built into the case as well. Scissors will also come in handy for opening those pesky vacuum-sealed plastic packaging.

Flashlight and Tray (for small parts). All the better to see you with, my dear.

Anti-Static Wristband. This is a wristband that grounds your body by keeping you in contact with the CPU's case at all times. Electrostatic discharge isn't common (unless you're on a carpet, or you're moving around too much) but if it happens it can render even the most expensive PC parts useless. If you don't have these wristbands, at least touch your PC's metal case with your bare hands every once in a while to keep yourself grounded and get rid of any built-up static electricity.

Finally, make sure you'll be building your PC on a flat, even, and **uncarpeted** surface. Carpets create a lot of static electricity that can fry your parts even before you can put them together!

SAFETY FIRST!

Now that you have the parts and tools, don't just go haphazardly putting them together! Make sure you have a well-lit, well-ventilated working area (again, no carpets!). Keep all tools within reach, and be careful not to lose any small stuff like screws. Take time to read the manuals of the individual parts you purchased — this seems rote, but they're there for a reason (especially, don't skip the safety warnings!). And make sure you have no other hazards (no nearby water sources, falling hazards, strong wind sources, shock hazards, etc.) nearby.

And off we go!

There are several ways to build a PC, and the one I'm advocating here is the "in the case" build. This means mounting your motherboard in the case first before snapping the parts in. While others may find more freedom, flexibility, and visibility in putting the parts together outside the case, this can be dangerous since the motherboard is unsupported by the case's structure.

STEP 1: Remove the case cover. Lay your PC case down on a flat surface, and unscrew the side panel to open it. Make sure to touch the metal with your bare hands first, and to keep the screws together safely.

STEP 2: Line up and mount the motherboard. Your motherboard will come with standoffs that can be lined up into the case. Screw them securely, and fasten the motherboard on top. Depending on the case, you may have to use the screwdriver to punch out the rear plate (there will be a cutout) to replace it with the motherboard's own input-output plate. This is where the peripherals will be connected together.

STEP 3: Mount the CPU. The motherboard's square CPU socket has a hinge that you can lift through a latch or lever. Make sure **NOT** to handle the CPU roughly! Instead, pick it up by the sides and line it up against the markings on the socket. Typically, there's a triangle on the board's socket that tells you how to align the processor.

Place the processor down gently, then lower the socket cover and secure it with the latch or elver. Don't push down or press the CPU. Depending on the motherboard, the socket may have a hard piece of plastic protecting it that you have to remove first.

STEP 4: Mount the CPU Cooler. The process will greatly depend on your CPU, cooler, and motherboard. The only thing to keep in mind is to ensure that the cooler is installed directly atop the metal housing of the processor, with nothing between the two parts. Sometimes you may need to apply thermal paste on the back of the CPU.

Whatever cooler you have, you will need to plug in the cable to the motherboard's power connector. You may have to look closely to identify which cable header is meant for the cooler — this is usually marked with the word "fan" (e.g., SYS_FAN, CPUFAN). For specific instructions, refer to the cooler's manual.

STEP 5. Mount the PSU. Secure the PSU with the screws, then plug the largest cable bundle into the power connector on the motherboard. Then, plug the smaller connector (8-pin) into the CPU power connector.

Different PSUs will look differently, and so will their cables. Visit the product manual that came with your PSU and motherboard for more details on which cable goes where.

STEP 6. Mount the RAM. RAM slots have clips at either end that have to be pushed out to allow the mounting of the modules. Slot the modules in, and press them down firmly

— the clips should automatically be pushed back in to secure the RAM in place. Some slots require a bit of force to seat the modules correctly but make sure you're not flexing the body of the RAM while doing so.

STEP 7. Mount the Graphics Card. If you're just using the CPU's onboard graphics, you can skip this. Otherwise, you need to punch out another panel from the back of the case where the graphics card will sit. You can fit the graphics card slot on the motherboard through the PCI expansion slot usually found at the lower half. Line up, push down firmly and screw the card in place. If you're using a more powerful graphics card, you might have to connect it to the PSU's power connector.

STEP 8. Mount the Storage. There are different types of storage, each with a different way of connecting. Cases also have separate drive bays for separate types, though some are interchangeable — for example, a 3.5-inch drive bay can hold a 2.5-inch SSD with an adapter plate.

The exact way of connecting drives will depend on your case, so refer to its manual. If you have a modern hard drive, it connects via the SATA cable that comes bundled with it. The SATA cable allows data to flow from your drive to the motherboard.There will be a separate cable for the power, directly from the PSU.

Other drives, such as optical drives (for DVDs) are also mounted this way.

STEP 9. Mount Case Connections. Depending again on the case, your PC might come with preinstalled fans and other connections, especially towards the front panel. You will need to plug these connections to a separate header port on the motherboard (not the PSU) for them to work.

STEP 10. Close the case and check the power. Fix the side cover back on, put the screws back in place, and test your computer! If everything works, your computer should power on. You might want to connect only the most basic peripherals (monitor, keyboard, mouse) just to see if all basic functions are working. This way, it's easy to disassemble things again if you need to dive back into the case. And make sure to use the graphics card's ports when plugging your monitor in!

Huh... for all the fanfare that building a PC is hard, that didn't seem too much, did it? Only 10 steps! Indeed, putting together all the parts is the easiest part of PC-building since most connections are fairly intuitive, and those that are not intuitive are at least clearly marked. When all else fails, there's always the product-specific manuals to tide you over.

The most difficult part is still choosing the various PC parts. That's where the bloodiest of battles are waged. Should you go Intel or AMD for your CPU? Are AIO coolers worth it? Which parts should you splurge on? Which models are great starting points? These are the burning questions that will take up so much of your PC-building time that actually working on the PC itself becomes a breeze. Thankfully, I have answers for these questions (and MUCH more) as well — but you'll have to wait until the next chapter!

Perhaps next most difficult is making sure that your custom-built PC actually *looks* like a custom-built PC, and not something fished out of a dumpster. Cable management plays a huge role in that. Tame the spaghetti wires by making sure that you plan where they're going before plugging them in, not just haphazardly connecting headers. You may need to bundle up longer cables or reroute them behind the motherboard. Make use of any cable management tool built into the case (some have cutouts or dedicated routes for wires), and make sure the bundle of cables isn't covering any of the vents or fans. You can also use twist ties, zip ties, or velcro strips to make sure the wires stay in a place where you want them,

Note that this guide has been built around the easiest and most straightforward way of building a PC. In case you have additional components you'd like to include (such as additional RGB lighting, because it's a free world and you can RGB anything), you can just add them before fixing the case cover back on.

The guide also applies even if you're building a PC out of older parts, though some things may change slightly. For example, you might be dealing with a motherboard that isn't as clearly marked, so you'd have to consult the manual more often (if it's pre-owned with no manual, there's always YouTube). If you have older drives, you may also be dealing with a bulkier IDE cable system, which installs differently from SATA. Make sure your motherboard supports IDE cables if you're going this way. And don't scoff at using pre-owned or refurbished stuff for your PC — part of the awesomeness of building your own PC is being able to choose the most cost-effective parts.

As with most things, the best way to build a PC when you're on a budget is to start small, with just basic parts, with a view towards an upgrade. This way if you end up making a mistake, it won't be expensive.

Something's not working!

Did your PC not turn on? Did it output a series of beeps instead of a picture? Here are a few things that could set you on the right track.

If nothing at all happens upon hitting the "on" switch...

- Make sure all components are connected to the power source, and that the PC is properly plugged into the outlet. Also check that the power supply's switch is turned on.
- Make sure there are no stray pieces of metal on and under the motherboard, which may ground it and cause it to not power on.
- Try a different power supply, if you're using an old one.

If the PC appears to turn on then dies after a second...

- If the fan shuts down, check if you were able to properly seat it on the CPU.
- If you are stuck in a boot loop (system turning on and off) then the RAM may not be properly mounted. There may also be an issue with the power supply not being enough to power the RAM, GPU, and various components. Finally, your motherboard may be broken.
- If your PC is beeping before spontaneously rebooting, take note of the beep pattern and Google the list of PC diagnostic codes — these are error messages outputted through beeps that gives you a clear idea of where the problem lies.
- If the system hangs then reboots, you may have an issue with a faulty RAM.

And remember, Google, YouTube, and Reddit's PC Gaming subreddit are your friends. Just type in your parts and a description of the issue you're having. This goes applies to any and every issue you're having, whether you're just starting out or booting up!

Now that you've turned your PC on, you're ready to... oh, wait. You get the BIOS screen? No startup sequence?

Of course, you don't have the OS installed yet. But that's a breeze, so let's get on with it!

Installing Windows

Windows is very easy to install but not that easy to buy. Simply because it's not free — and though there are several places out there where you can get a bootlegged copy of Windows, I would recommend nothing short of buying an actual license. Having one ensures you get continuous updates and protection for the lifespan of the OS.

You can get genuine Windows as CDs from authorized retailers (you need an optical disc drive to install in this manner). You can also download the OS from Microsoft's website and create an installation media of your own, such as on a USB stick. You can install this without entering a product key, and purchase the product key separately though the Windows Store to make your install an authentic copy. When you download the OS, make sure you get the version that is right for your architecture! Modern PCs will work with 64-bit Windows, while older rigs might benefit better from a 32-bit OS, especially if you're working with 2GB of RAM or less.

Once you have your installation media, make sure the BIOS is set to boot it (usually by going to Boot Media or a similar option in the BIOS settings, then choosing the drive from which to boot) and insert or plug your media in. Then, follow these simple steps:

STEP 1. Choose your language, time zone, and keyboard layout. This will be on the first screen that appears when you start the install process.

STEP 2. Click **Install Now**. If you're using a downloaded copy of the Windows installer, you will be asked to enter a product key. As previously mentioned, you can defer this for later. You will have to accept Microsoft's License Terms in the next window, too.

STEP 3. If a screen pops up that asks you whether to install normally or do a custom install, you can select the latter only if you want to install Windows on a custom partition in your drive. Otherwise, go for a regular install which will turn your entire drive into a Windows drive.

STEP 4. Wait. The installation process will resume, during which the PC may automatically restart a few times.

STEP 5. Follow through with the set-up prompt. This will appear once Windows is installed, and can take a few minutes. The prompts take you everywhere from Cortana to the privacy settings. It also allows you to choose a secondary keyboard layout, a network connection, an associated email address, and more. If you're privacy-minded, you might want to turn off the plethora of tracking options that Microsoft has automatically enabled.

Once you're done, that's pretty much it! You now have a working PC, a loyal gaming machine ready to serve you at any moment. It was born from your hands, and it's completely yours. Nevermind if it's like Frankenstein's monster, built out of scrap and spare parts — you've earned an achievement, and have crossed a frontier that many others fear or fail to cross.

You're now a full-blooded member of the PC Master Race!

CHAPTER 7: The Burning Questions and Great Debates of PC Gaming (and Building)

Over the course of your life as a PC user (note, *user*, not just gamer or builder) you will encounter a raging torrent of VS debates on any and every conceivable topic. Some of them are a bit superficial, such as whether some recent change in a game update improves the story or detracts from it. Some are a little more important, such as whether to go Intel or AMD on your first build (Nvidia or AMD for the GPU) or what product to go for in a specific budget range. This chapter helps you answer all of these and more!

The CPU: Team Red or Team Blue?

This argument is just a whirly eddy of conflicting opinions, but here are my two cents — if you're gaming and building your own PC, go for Team Red (AMD). AMD's most recent line of Ryzen processors has more cores and threads than their Intel counterparts, making them faster. They are also easier to overclock (though they have far less overclocking headroom than Intel), have better compatibility with motherboards thanks to the AM4 socket (meaning you can upgrade more easily), and generally have more modern architectures.

This may come as a surprise since most PC users know that Intel's name stands for supreme processor quality, and indeed they have been closing the gap in the past few years. But barring any breakthroughs, AMD still has the most bang for the buck.

If gaming isn't your primary deal and you want your PC to be compatible with the widest possible variation of apps and use cases, then go Intel. Being the pioneer means they have built an entire ecosystem around them, so many apps are optimized to run on Intel devices. AMD's not far behind on this one, but Intel still wears the compatibility crown.

The Graphics Card: Team Red or Team Green?

The second-hottest flame war after Intel v AMD (and perhaps the hottest for gamers), this matchup sees a reversal of fortunes for Team Red. In a vast majority of games, Nvidia has the clear lead when it comes to optimization, and it even competes toe-to-toe with AMD's traditionally low prices in its newest lineup. Nvidia is also the leader in innovation, being the first company to produce cards that factor in ray tracing support. Nvidia cards also offer more feature technologies, with DirectX 12 Ultimate enhancements.

If you're strapped for cash though but would still like to have a discrete graphics card for your build, then AMD's entry-level options would be a decent choice. They offer better value than the more premium cards of Team Green, and they still pack a decent punch.

But here's a twist — unlike with CPUs, there actually are other companies that create decent graphics cards! You'd encounter one of them in our recommendations later on.

The Storage: Hard drive or Solid state?

We've already discussed a little of the differences that make up the two, and for most gaming purposes SSDs are the way to go. Games need to be stored in a high-capacity drive that allows lightning-fast data retrieval and storage, and SSDs can dance circles around traditional hard drives in the speed department. Unlike CPUs and GPUs, though, it's not an either-or debate so you can still have an HDD (which can store more data for the dollar than SSDs) for other media or as secondary storage. Also, beware that HDDs require more power than SSDs.

Which specific parts should I buy for my build?

This would, of course, largely depend on your budget and your vision for your PC. But here are a few gaming-oriented parts per budget range.

Case:
Budget. Go for the Corsair Carbide 275R, which is just a little above $100 and offers all the basics of a great case — good motherboard support, sleek dimensions, cool looks, and a lot of room for parts and fans. There's also a good array of I/O ports for all your peripherals. If you want something smaller, you can go for the NZXT H210i case which is almost similar in all respects except that it only accepts a Mini-ITX motherboard.

Mid-Range. Among the best PC cases anywhere is the Cooler Master Cosmos C700P. It's big and heavy, and triple the price of our budget recommendation. But it's also the perfect canvas for your dream PC build, as its spacious interior lets it take just about anything you can throw into it, even those oversized parts.

High-End. This case isn't for the faint of heart. It's HUGE ("super-tower case" isn't an exaggeration), with a price tag to match (above $500). But it's so over the top you can put TWO PC builds inside it! Yes, people actually do that, and quite regularly. There's also space for 18 fans, in case you're wondering if all that heat wouldn't melt the case.

Motherboard:

Budget. If you're going for an AMD build, and are looking for a motherboard with an AM4 socket, the best budget selection would be MSI's MAG B550M Mortar. Priced under $200, the B550M allows the Ryzen chip to unleash its full potential, while also offering the possibility of easy upgrades.

If you're looking for an Intel 10th Gen-capable motherboard, then ASRock's B460 Steel Legend gives the most bang for the buck with its similar sub-$200 price tag and hefty features.

If you're looking for a Mini-ITX motherboard, one of the best entry-level ones is the sub-$100 Gigabyte A520 Aorus Elite. It also offers an AM4 socket that allows for excellent upgradeability.

Mid-Range. For a mid-range AMD PC build, you'd want to consider MSI's MPG X570 — considered as one of the best motherboards overall for Ryzen CPUs. It's got perfect compatibility with the current and future crop of mid-to high-end components, and it doesn't break the bank. It's also just under $300, so no need to break out your life savings.

Similarly priced on the 10th Gen Intel side is the MSI MPG Z490 Gaming Carbon WiFi. It's nothing luxurious, but it provides the perfect mix of value and features that can handle all but the most aggressive Intel CPUs of today. And while an overclocked i9 might cause cooling problems, its lesser siblings will cruise just fine.

High-End. For the price of these motherboards, you can actually build a full PC or two! AMD fans can splurge for the sub-$700 Asus ROG Crosshair VIII Dark Hero, which is the optimal choice if you're also splurging for an AMD Ryzen 5000 series CPU as well. It's so powerful and easy to use that it has gained quite a following amongst AMD PC builders.

For Intel, there's the legendary Asus ROG Maximus XII Extreme, which has all the bells, whistles, and builds quality you can ever expect for a $1,000 motherboard. It's powerful enough to handle the fastest overclocked Intel CPU you can find anywhere if that's your thing!

CPU:

Warning: for the reasons mentioned earlier in this chapter, it's all AMD Ryzen on this list!

Budget. If budget is a constraining consideration, you can go with the Ryzen 3 3300X. It's good enough for gaming, allowing your PC to handle great games in mid-range graphics settings. But if you can push for at least the Ryzen 5 3600X for much higher performance.

Mid-Range. The Ryzen 5 5600X is among the best overall CPUs for gamers, with the perfect blend of price and performance. Indeed, most gamers could get away with playing AAA games with this little beast, and there'll still be enough power left for streaming.

High-End. If you really want to push it, there are hundreds of ways to overkill your CPU. But for our purposes, you can just go with the Ryzen 9 5950X with a whipping of 16 cores and 32 threads. Make sure you have the right coolers to match this one!

GPU:

Unlike with CPUs, you can't really put an all-Nvidia line-up on this one for a simple reason — Nvidia doesn't really have a "budget" segment that can equal our recommendation below.

Budget. You don't have to spend several hundred on a GPU. In fact, you just need around $150 for the XFX RX 570 GPU (4GB), and you can game on your merry way! This card isn't the best for high-performance systems, but it can take you through a buttery-smooth HD gaming performance without breaking the bank.

Mid-Range. Here's where Nvidia comes in, with the sub-$700 GeForce RTX 3060 Ti. Very affordable, as far as GPUs go — and very capable, too! Even for more graphically demanding games, you won't need much more than this.

High-End. If you want to have something that can run anything the gaming industry can throw at it (even for the foreseeable future), look no further than the sub-$3,000 Nvidia GeForce RTX 3080. It's pretty rare, and for a good reason. Make sure you have enough power from the PSU for this beast!

RAM:

Budget. RAMs, despite their importance in a PC, are a heck of a lot cheaper than other components. And it doesn't get much cheaper than OLOy Owl, which gives you great speed under $100.

Mid-Range. G.Skill is a well-known name, and its Ripjaws V series offers a great balance on cost and performance. In fact, for the same speed and capacity, Ripjaws V is even more affordable than many of its competitors.

High-End. If you have money to burn, try this RAM module that costs as much like a CPU. The Corsair Dominator Platinum RGB doesn't just have an awesome name, it also has some of the absolute best RAM performance anywhere in the market.

PSU:

Budget. Gaming PSUs have a higher capacity than non-gaming ones, so they're necessarily more expensive. Still, you can keep to your budget with the Cooler Master MasterWatt 750W. It has semi-modular cables, too, so cable management can be a lot easier.

Mid-Range. Corsair provides a lot of quality PC goodies, and their RM850x PSUs certainly fit the bill. These power supplies are known for their efficiency and reliability, which are both critical for PSUs.

High-End. Seasonic Prime 1000 Titanium. Just the name inspires a hefty price tag, and indeed you can buy two entry-level PCs for the price of this 1000W PSU. Fully modular, top-quality build, and incredibly reliable — you get what you pay for.

Storage Drives:

We're sticking to SSDs on this front since they'll be the primary drivers of your system. If you're custom building a modern gaming PC, HDDs should only serve as secondary memory banks. Also, note that SSDs come in various form factors — but built correctly they can all be used as your OS drives.

Budget. The best balance of speed, reliability, and price comes in the small package of the Samsung 860 Evo. This SATA3 SSD has some of the best-read and write speeds in the sub-$60 price range, and it can be a good foundation for a first-time PC build.

Mid-Range. Intel is also in the storage arena, and its 760p Series drives are some of the best when it comes to read speeds. Leveraging the power of NVMe, this SSD is perfect for a snappy OS drive if you have around $200 to spare.

High-End. A little less than $300 at its most expensive, Samsum tops the list in both price and quality with the 970 Pro SSD. It is among the fastest SSDs you will find anywhere, and unlike Intel's offering is not biased towards read speed. It's fit to be part of any powerful PC build, no matter the use case.

Cooler:

Okay, before we move to the recommendations let's address the little Air v Liquid cooling debate. CPU coolers are very important because the CPU generates *lots* of heat, and without them your PC's core would turn into a molten slab. Air coolers use fans to move away the hot air from the CPU itself, while liquid coolers use a liquid coolant to absorb the heat from the CPU. Liquid coolers are divided into AIO (All-In-One) and custom cooling loops, but the latter requires much more know-how and experience to set up.

By nature, air coolers are much more simple and hence cost much less. They are also easier to install, though not by a wide margin. Furthermore, air coolers take up less overall space than AIOs.

However, liquid cooling is quieter and much more efficient than air cooling, so if you need an external cooler (i.e., the CPU you bought did not have its own cooler) and you spend a lot of time gaming, you need to seriously consider AIO cooling. Because of this, we're focusing on AIO coolers for this section.

Budget. You can't go wrong with an EVGA CLC 240, especially if you're not the type to leave your PC on and crunching numbers the whole day. These coolers have great performance at a sub-$100 price point. Be warned that the fans can get a little loud, though.

Mid-Range. Cooler Master has another entry, with the MasterLiquid ML360R. This one features a larger-than-life radiator that allows it to cool your jets without kicking up a storm. It's also priced below $200, so it's great for the quality.

High-End. Also in the sub-$200 category, the Corsair H115i RGB Platinum is among the best liquid coolers anywhere. It's pretty, it's quiet, and it's efficient enough to let you unleash your rig's full potential.

Monitor:

Whoo boy, this one's difficult. Simply put, there's a bajillion monitors around from various manufacturers, and choosing one really depends on your individual preferences even more than your budget. It's also influenced by the games you play (better picture, or faster refresh?), your GPU (FreeSync or G-Sync), and many others.

So instead of making outright recommendations here (which could be easily meaningless in the light of variations in preference), let me just give a few pointers on how to choose monitors.

- In gaming, bigger is not always better. Not all games can support scaling very well, so having too big a monitor with a high pixel density means having small in-game elements. A 27-inch monitor should be big enough for most purposes.
- The bigger the monitor, the higher the resolution you should aim for. Typically, a 24-inch monitor should work well on 1080p. At bigger sizes, though, this resolution is just underwhelming.
- We've already given pointers on refresh rates and other specs in Chapter 5, but let me reiterate this tip — don't get blindsided by empty marketing terms, such as impossible contrast ratios!
- You might want to check out ultra-wide screens as well (21:9) ratio, but be warned that not all games support the format.

Other Peripherals:

There are lots of other things that can be added to your PC. If the motherboard does not have its own WiFi card installed, for example, you might want to install a separate WiFi card for wireless connections. It's also possible to add USB ports to the motherboard through a USB expansion card in PCI slots. You may add DVD/BluRay drives, SD card readers, Bluetooth cards and more — all depending on your preference.

How often should I clean my PC?

There are lots of apps to clean garbage in your PC, but how about its physical form? There are those who set-and-forget their PCs until they encounter errors, only to find out that the PC case has become the haunt of dust, spiders, and other creatures of darkness.

As a rule, any foreign particle that enters your PC has the potential to damage it. Even dust particles can hamper your PC's performance by impeding the air flow that's necessary in order to cool down your PC's internals.

While there are cases that have integrated dust traps and other features that isolate the internals from foreign particles, it's still a must to clean your PC. Give it a good wipe down (while powered off and disconnected from the power outlet!) every couple of weeks, and crack the case open at least once a quarter to clean out anything that might have gotten in. Do this more frequently if you're in a high-dust area. A can of compressed air can be your best friend in this endeavor.

The OS Wars: Why not Mac or Linux?

There's no beating around the bush here — Mac is just way too expensive and elitist, and Linux is just way too geeky. Don't get me wrong, I realize both these OSes have a lot of things going for them (Mac's finesse and stability, Linux's supreme flexibility) but only Windows has hit that sacred middle ground in terms of user-friendliness and openness.

Of course, it's possible to game with both Mac and Linux. Especially in recent years, Linux devs have implemented various ways to make the OS gamer-friendly, with Steam even creating a full-blown SteamOS distro around it, specially built for living room gaming. This adds to the penguin's prowess, helping it get away from the notion that Linux gaming is all about Raspberry Pi-built emulators for modern arcade cabinets (yes, Linux emulates really well and most of its gaming is centered on this). But neither Mac nor Linux boasts the massive catalog of games that Windows has. Couple that with the OS's support and there's simply no other option for desktop (or laptop) gaming.

Should I Stream?

You've seen these people — those who do commentaries, rants, reviews, recommendations, and everything in between while playing a game. In a way, streaming divides the gaming community. While many of us love watching those walkthroughs and reviews, there are also a few who think that streaming reduces and commercializes the gaming lifestyle — especially since there are so many "gamers" out there who stream without really knowing what they're doing.

Still, streaming is always an option — and even more, it's a possibly lucrative means of income. Streamers earn from one of two main methods: sponsorships/partnerships, and "tips" (and similar income) from stream subscribers or viewers. Streakers can also earn from ads, affiliate links, or even selling their own merchandise!

To get started, here are a few basics about streaming based on the top platforms:

Twitch. Considered the prime gamer streaming service, Twitch offers several ways of earning. First, there are subscriptions — when your fans subscribe to your Twitch channel, you get 50% of their monthly fees as revenue

(Twitch gets the other half). Your channel can be eligible for subscribers if you have at least 50 followers, after which you can apply to be a Twitch Affiliate.

Others, especially those who don't make it as Affiliates, tend to use third-party services like Patreon so that they can collect the full monthly subscription fees.

Fans can also purchase "Bits" (a sort of glorified emoticon) and send them to the streamer. Since they are bought with real money, sending them also has a real money equivalent — for every 100 Bits received by a streamer, they earn a dollar.

And of course, there are donations, ads, sponsorships, and more!

YouTube. The second most popular game streaming site after Twitch, streaming on Facebook is as simple as pressing a Go Live button. Monetization isn't that easy, though, since you will need to be part of the YouTube Partner Program. This means you need to have at least a *thousand* subscribers and a total of 4,000 watch hours in the past year. If you have reached these levels, though, you can start enabling ads on your stream (you know those videos that run before and in the middle of videos?). As a gaming channel, you can also unlock Channel Memberships to allow users to support you with a monthly fee.

Facebook Gaming. Rounding up the trinity of game streaming is Facebook. And just as with anything on this social media giant, sharing a game stream is very easy. All you need is to create a page categorized as a Gaming Video Creator, and you're ready to start.

Facebook Gaming has its own Level Up Program that allows you to monetize your content. There are separate milestones (a hundred followers, for starters) that you need to reach, but it's generally not as steep as YouTube's.

Regardless of the platform you choose (and you can choose all of them — some services like Streamlabs Prime lets you stream to all three at once), you will need a few basic tools before you can stream.

A good PC. This is a no-brainer. Stream with a low-end PC and you're likely to suffer from debilitating lags and crashes. Ideally (but not necessarily), your PC should also have a capture card that will ease the load on your system and facilitate the streaming of on-screen content at high resolutions. There are even some cards that will let you combine images from multiple sources (such as your screen and your webcam) for an all-in-one solution. There are also capture cards that work with consoles! For starters, look up Elgato's lineup of cards.

The right software. There are several streaming apps with widely varying features at your disposal. Some of them do the work of capture cards and combine the inputs of several different sources. Others allow for more high-tech features such as green screens, social media ad integration, stream + record, special effects, and more. Some, on the other hand, specialize in the simplest task of just recording screens.

You don't necessarily have to pay for streaming software. The famous Open Broadcast Software (OBS) can be downloaded for free. Of course, you can splurge and instead go for a full-blown professional streaming software like vMix... for over a thousand bucks. But there are lots of options in between, so take your pick!

Enough technical know-how. Being a streamer isn't all about knowing the game. You also need to know your way around the software you're using, and how they integrate into the services you're using. You also need to know basic hardware troubleshooting, as you don't want glitches cramping your style.

But perhaps even more important than the technical know-how will be the *non*-technical stuff, i.e. how well you interact with people on your stream. A streamer's business and reputation are built not just by how well he plays, but by how well he entertains the people who watch him. This is why you'll find Twitch streamers who put in the effort to create emotes for their subscribers, and those who give away freebies. They interact directly through chat and sometimes open up other channels like Discord. They take time to recognize the viewers and supporters and even set up their pages and streams for maximum entertainment. Streaming is, in all its practical points, a part of the entertainment industry — showmanship is a must!

In recent years the streaming market has grown tremendously, pioneered by such figures as PewDiePie, Markiplier, and JackSepticEye. Because of the torrent of content coming from aspiring streamers, some game publishers have seen it fit to block monetization (yeah, I know) for certain games. This is something you need to be aware of, so do a quick search of the games you'd like to stream and see if they have a broadcast license. If there is, you're good to go... and if you charm audiences, who knows if you're the next Ninja! Just... make sure not to get sucked in by all the drama that the streaming life has in spades.

CONCLUSION

And there you have it! By now you already know everything there is about gaming on the PC — from its history to its evolution, from its fundamentals to the nitty-gritty. Heck, you've even learned how to build your own PC from scratch, which many people can't even boast about!

As I've said earlier, a PC is an incredibly multi-faceted tool. So while we have built the PC with gaming as a primary end, know that your membership in the PC Master Race has also opened the door to a massive set of opportunities. Anything as powerful as a gaming PC should also be powerful enough to handle the tough workloads of whatever profession or business you're in. The PC can be used as a tool for developing pretty much anything, and as a platform from white you can bring your own creations to the world. The skills you may learn from gaming or streaming may also be transferable to other areas of your life. Take pride in your games, and in your mad skillz.

It's my sincerest hope that with this book, you're not just able to learn about the glorious PC Master Race and its different facets, but that you've earned skills and knowledge you can apply anywhere else. This has been a fulfilling journey for me, and I hope that it is the same for you.

And remember, technology as a whole and the gaming landscape in particular are continuously evolving! In a year or two, many of the things you've read here may have taken on different forms. Maybe RetroArch will evolve to be able to emulate every console there is on the market. Maybe even more powerful graphics cards, cable systems, and monitors can be built, so you don't need to choose between max picture quality and max refresh rate. Maybe ray-tracing will become the norm. Maybe (or rather, surely?) the price of PC parts will go down so everyone can enjoy at least mid-level gaming on a budget. What's written here reflect the current realities of PC gaming (in 2021), but the future is coming in at breakneck speeds.

So don't get left behind! Even when things have changed, your fellow gamers will be here to lend a hand. Ask question in Reddit, search out new ideas and solutions in Google and YouTube. The PC Master Race will always have your back. They will help you, just as they have helped me in the past!

Now that you have your finger on the pulse of the PC gaming world, keep it there and stay amazed at the cutting-edge developments the future may bring!

Finally, I would like to ask a little favor of you now that you've finished this book. If you'd be so kind, please leave me a review about how this book has helped or impacted you in any way. These reviews help me a lot, and it helps keep me churning out more quality content!

Until next time, and just like the PC — keep evolving!

www.ingramcontent.com/pod-product-compliance
Lightning Source LLC
LaVergne TN
LVHW041210050326
832903LV00021B/562